PRACTICAL WICCA CANDLE SPELLS FOR BEGINNER WICCANS

A newbies guide to picking candles, setting mindset, prepping, spells plus candle recipes

SHEILA DEVINA PALTROW

Silk Publishing

INTRODUCTION

I would like to thank you for choosing this book to help you expand your magical practice. I hope you get plenty of enjoyment out of this book, and I hope you find it helpful, whatever your goals may be.

Whether we know it or not, candles play a very big role in Wiccans' spiritual practice Candles are a great tool to set the mood and to direct energies, so they often get used in most spells. This book is here to provide you with a thorough knowledge of candle magic and how you can make your spiritual practice even more powerful with them.

The first thing we are going to cover is what candle magic is all about. This is going to give you a basic understanding of this type of magic and why it is something that all Wiccans should understand. You will also learn that you have been practicing some form of candle magic for a while now.

Then we are going to go over some of the best ways to pick your candles. While this is not that complicated of a process, you must know what the different colors mean and the different sizes you can pick from.

Next, we will go over how you can work your candle magic in

INTRODUCTION

time with the moon phases. Every phase of the moon will give you a different form of energy, and while you don't have to time your spells with these phases, it will increase their power if you do.

After that, we will look at how to create your own anointing oils that you can use to dress your candles. Most of the time, your candles should be anointed with some sort of oil, and what better oil to use than homemade oil that has your mojo coursing through it?

Then we will go over the best ways to use your candles. This is going to look at the proper practices of dressing and inscribing candles for the most power. This is sometimes intimidating, but it is actually very simple.

Next, we will go over how to grow your candle collection so that you are prepared for any magic work you need to do. This is especially helpful if you plan on performing candle magic on a regular basis. Candles come in all shapes, sizes, and colors, so it's a good idea to have a few of each on hand.

Then you will find a chapter full of spells that you can perform with your candles. It's important, though, that you have a clear intention in mind before you start doing any of these spells.

Lastly, you will find a little bonus. There will be five recipes for how to create your own magic candles.

Once again, thank you for choosing this book. There are many books on this subject out there, so thanks for choosing mine.

CHAPTER 1
THE POWER OF FIRE

Many people have said that candle magic is the oldest form of magic in the history of humans. It doesn't matter if this is true or not; indeed, fire has always been sacred to our pagan ancestors who supplicated and honored their gods with candles, torches, flaming wheels, and balefires. Since the fire was the only source of light other than the moon and sun until the early 1900s, it is easy to see why fire is a symbol of power throughout history.

Being reverent to fire has continued for a long time, even after modern lighting caught on. Today, most religions still use candles, whether in a formal service or when lighting a votive for certain intentions.

Candle magic is the easiest way to cast spells, and because of this, it doesn't take many ceremonial or ritual tools. Basically, anybody who has a candle could cast a spell. Remember back to when you had a birthday party as a child. You always made a wish before you blew out your candles. This is the same idea behind candle magic. Rather than just "hoping" that your wish comes true, you will be declaring your intent. Nobody remembers where that tradition originated from and won't remember who came up with the notion of using candles for magic.

There is something very pleasant about watching the flicker of a candle flame. It makes us feel at ease and peaceful when you look into that living, dancing, flickering light. Lighting a candle is the easiest way to begin shifting out of this reality, and connecting with all the unseen energies that are around us all the time. It doesn't matter if you want to cause a spell or not.

Candle spells are straightforward, elegant, and simple. They can help you strengthen and build your "magic muscles" or your ability to direct and focus your energy on your intentions. It is the powerful thoughts that are underneath both the simple and most complex types of magic.

Magic is an art form that sends a specific thought out into the spiritual plane where it gets manifested and then returned back to you on the Earthly plane. For people who are just beginning, candles are great messengers. The request that you are making is being sent through the flame. This request is called an intention. The flame is the medium here. While the candle burns, it will leave the material plane and goes into the ethereal one. It carries your intention with it. If you are a beginner to magic, this example can help you visualize the process.

Think about that birthday candle again for a moment. That ritual is based on three principles:

- Figure out a goal
- Imagine the end result you want
- Focus your will or intent to make the result happen

WHY DO CANDLE MAGIC?

If candle magic is so simple, why do we even need to practice it? People who are new to magic might think they can get more magic out of a complicated spell. Candle magic can actually be very powerful, even though it is so simple. This is because candle magic harnesses transformative power: fire, wax, and wick.

When you do candle magic, you are harnessing fire's power to bring about some sort of change. Think about how fire can change things. It can melt the wax. It can turn a lot of organic materials like bone, flesh, wood, and leaves into ash. It can soften hard materials to make them malleable. This helps you change it into whatever you would like. It can heat up substances and turn them from a liquid into gas like water into steam. If you mix different ingredients together and then put them into the fire, it can change your dough into a loaf of bread or your batter into a cake. It can bring you warmth when you are cold and light when it is dark.

Ever since humans discovered fire, we have been in awe of its power. We have tried to harness this power to use its transformative powers. We are continuing this tradition every time we do candle magic.

That moment you start planning any spell, you have started the process of casting. Remember to keep your intentions good along with a positive attitude since you are pouring your energy into your goal.

The candle isn't the power source. The wick and wax isn't the driver behind the magic; it is the fire that burns the wick and melts the wax.

THE BASICS

This might seem odd, but the candle isn't the power source when doing candle magic. The wick and wax are the drivers of the magic but the fire that is burning the wick and wax.

Think back to all those birthdays. The wish didn't work, did it? This is because you blew the candles out. During candle magic, you shouldn't blow out the candles. You have to let the candles burn out by themselves or extinguish them with wet fingers or a toll. When you blow out candles, the element sees this as an insult.

Balance of the Elements

Since it is a symbolic object, the candle is a great representation of the Elements. The base and wick of the candle is representative of the element Earth. This is needed to keep the flame lit and grounded. The wax that turns from a solid into a liquid and then to gas has the element water characteristics. Air is found in the oxygen, which is also needed to keep the flame lit. The flame is, of course, the element Fire. The element Spirit or Akasha comes when you charge your candle with your intention. Then you have a tool that embodies the whole Universe in one little package.

Picking a Candle

Many practitioners of magic are going to tell you that the size of your candle doesn't matter. The truth is that larger candles might be counterproductive. If a candle takes three days to burn completely, it can be distracting to somebody who is trying to work a spell that needs the candle to burn out completely.

Basically, you can use whatever candle you want to in your spells. But most Witches will use tapers. Table candles are available almost everywhere. They don't have to be put into a candlestick, and they can burn for around eight hours and could be used in many spells. It would be a good idea to keep some of these on hand. You can use chime candles if you have to. Tea lights can be used, but they are hard to anoint. Pillar candles work well for multi-day spells, but they are a waste for a one day spell.

Normally a short taper or votive candle is going to work the best. You might come across a spell that calls for a certain type of sympathetic or a seven-day candle. This most popular candle is the small menorah candles that are sold by the box. You can find these in the kosher section of any grocery store. These are around four inches long, thin, unscented, and white. This makes them perfect for working spells.

You need to make sure you use a new candle for every spell. Don't use candles that you have burned in the bathroom or on your dining room table. According to tradition, candles can pick up vibrations from the things around them when it begins to burn. If vibrations have already tainted a candle, some think that it could cause ineffective or negative outcomes to your spells.

Other types of candles include:

- Container candles
- Figurine candles: pyramids, skulls, animals, lovers, male and female parts, crosses
- Votives
- Seven knob candles: wishing candle
- Tea lights
- Novena: these are called vigil or seven-day candles
- Chime candles
- Birthday candles: these are wonderful for quick spells

You should be able to find your candles at most stores, and these are great, but if you want your spell to have some pizzazz, you might want to consider getting some spell candles.

Color Magic

In addition to the excellent symbolic qualities, candles let us work with the magic of colors in a focused and direct way. For hundreds of years, colors have been associated with specific events or qualities such as luck, death, wealth, and love. Red has always represented passion and love. It is the color of blood and the heart. Green has always represented abundance because of the green color of the Earth during the growing season.

Using these colors in your candle magic can help reinforce your intention, and the candles are designed for this particular purpose. These are usually called "spell candles" and can be found in any color you can think of.

Cleansing Your Candle

You have purchased your candles, you have created your goals, and you have designed your spell. You are ready to begin, right?

No, you aren't.

Before you light any candle that you will be using in a spell, you have to cleanse it first. This gives your magic the best results possible. You don't want all the energies of the people who have touched it before you.

An easy way you can do this is to smudge the candle. You can do this the same way you smudge your house. If you don't have access to a smudge stick, you could use a purification ritual or spray, incense smoke, or smudge spray.

Charge and Bless the Candle

Once you have cleansed your candle, you need to seal in good intentions and bless it. There are a few ways you can do this:

1. Say a prayer while holding the candle or chant an incantation that is related to your goals.
2. Breathe your energy into the candle. Imagine your breath encircling the candle and infusing it.
3. Put both hands on the candle and imagine your energy seeping into the candle. You could imagine a bright light moving from your hands and into your candle.

Preparing Your Altar

Find a space in your home. It could be just a nightstand or a small table. Using a paper towel and water, wipe down the table area that you are going to use for your altar in a counter-clockwise motion. While you are cleaning, think about your intention and push your energy into this space. Place your candle into a holder along with everything else that will represent the work you are getting ready to do on your altar so that it is pleasing to you.

Using a Candle in Rituals

Once you have cleansed and charged your candle and

prepared your altar, you will need to dress or oil the candle before you burn it. This is done to create a psychic link between the candle and you. It will also push your intent into the candle before you light it. During this time, you need to imagine your intent and put your energy into it. You can do the chant at this time if you would like. You might begin to feel the energy building. Your hands might feel like they are tingling, or the candle might begin to feel as if it is pulsing. These are all good things. It means it is working. You might have to do this for a few minutes until you "know" that the candle has been completely charged. You can choose to dress your candle beforehand or right before you cast your spell.

The type of candle magic that is the most basic uses pieces of colored paper that will match your intent. You have first to figure out what your goal is and then write it on that piece of paper.

If you want to work with money, your intent might be: "I will be financially prosperous." Some traditions might require that you write down your intent in a magical alphabet like the Enochian or Theban. Since this is a money spell, you should choose either a green or gold piece of paper with a candle of the same color. As you are writing down your goal, imagine yourself reaching that goal.

Visualize various ways that your goal could manifest, like making more money at work. Maybe somebody who owes you money will repay their debt to you. You might get a huge tax refund.

When you have written your goal down, fold the paper, and stay focused on your intent the entire time. You could say an incantation while you do this. You don't have to do anything fancy. It can be this simple:

"Extra money come my way. I could use some cash today. Extra money comes to me, as I will so it shall be."

Put one corner of the paper into the flame of the candle and let it catch on fire. Hold onto the paper as long as you can. Just don't burn your fingers. Place it in or on a cauldron or a fireproof bowl and let it burn completely. Let the candle burn completely, too. Once the candle has melted, get rid of it instead of saving it to be used again. There usually isn't much left except a little stub of wax. You can either bury it outside or throw it away in any way you would like.

When you have finished, remember to thank your god and the elements and let them go. A great closing phrase would be: "Go if you must, stay if you will, but know that you are always welcome."

Figure Out Your Goal

As with any magical work, it is extremely important to add thoughts to your goals. You could do an unfocused spell, and it might work, but it might not work in the way you think it will or that you would want. Keep these tips in mind when you set a goal:

- Specific: Never use the word "wish" when making your goals
- Realistic: You aren't going to be able to create a million dollars, but you might motivate yourself to work harder. Don't let yourself wander into the fantasy realm
- Ethical: You always have to act ethically. Never interfere with a person's free will.
- Keep Language Positive: Stay away from words such as "not," "won't," "can't," and "don't." Give yours wants a direction to go. Don't cut off any avenues of growth.
- Create many goals: Break large goals down into smaller, easily managed ones.

Keeping these tips in mind, write down your goal into one sentence like: "I need to earn money to pay my car insurance." or "I want to be protected from harm on my travels."

Designing the Spell

Use the goal that you created to help you design your spell. Let's say you want to do a spell to help bring money for your car insurance. Let's do the most basic spell: "Visualize your goal and light a candle to release the energy."

It is best if you can keep your components at a minimum and simple. You just need a taper candle with a holder, oils to dress your candle, and some spices and herbs for power.

You need to chant to raise some energy. You can use any chant that you can find online, or you can make one up yourself. The most important thing about the chant is that it means something to you. I like using rhymes since they are easy to get a rhythm going and easy to remember.

If you like to use moon magic, you will need to check a lunar calendar to figure out the best planetary hour or which moon sign to do you spell.

A Chant to Attract Money

Here is a chant from my college days when I was trying to pay off my loans, get my career going, and to get my finances in order:

"Money, money come to me. I seize this opportunity. With this spell, the tables turn. What I need is what I earn. Increased paychecks I will see; this is my will, so mote it be!"

Collecting the Components

Try to choose components that will be in line with your

goals. You will need to find a candle the color you need along with oils, spices, and herbs that are also in line with your goals. For this money spell, a spell has already been designed to use one candle, one holder, oil, spices, and herbs. Let's find out how to choose the right components that will align themselves to your spell.

You will need:

- A Gold Candle Holder: Gold is representative of wealth. It doesn't have to be real gold; a holder that is just a gold color will be fine.
- Green Candle: This needs to be a new candle that hasn't been burnt at all. For picking out the right color, we will go over that in a later chapter.
- Ground Ginger: This versatile spice helps to speed up the results.
- Dragon's Blood: This is a resin the gives power to your spells.
- Ground Cinnamon: This potent spice has been associated with wealth.
- Patchouli Oil: Has been associated with prosperity.

Picking Your Components

A big part of learning how to do spells is learning to choose components that are appropriate for your goal. There are many charts on the internet and in books that will tell you what you need. Even though these charts could be helpful, you need to remember that components need to have special meanings for you.

A good thing to ask when picking out your components is: "What things do I associate with my goal?" If working with a money spell, green is associated with wealth and money. If red, brown, or gold remind you of wealth and money, you can use those colors instead. If you don't have any essential oils, you can use corn oil. Corn is reminiscent of prosperity and cash crops. You could also use olive oil, since it is a bit pricier, so you can view it as a luxury.

Ginger is great to use to speed up the results of your spells. If you don't like the smell of Asian foods, and smelling ginger reminds you of Asian foods, then don't use it.

Adding Power to Your Spells

- Spices and Herbs

It was stated earlier that you could add spices and herbs to add some power to yourself. You might be wondering how to do that. It's actually fairly simple. Once you have chosen the spices and herbs that you want to use, charge them with your intent by holding them in your hand. After you have dressed your candle, you can sprinkle them over or roll the candle in the spices.

- Symbols and Runes

You can also add power by scratching a symbol, number, or name into the candle. You can use a knife, earring, pin, or anything you have on hand to scratch it into your candle.

For a money spell, you can scratch your name into the wax. You could also use the ancient rune Fehu that symbolizes prosperity.

If runes don't mean anything to you, you can pick a different symbol like a money bag or dollar sign. You could write the word "money" onto the candle, too.

· · ·

Casting the Spell

Once it is time to cast your spell, sit in front of your candle, and do the following:

- Meditate for as long as you need in order to get relaxed. Take some deep breaths, release any tension from your body, and let go of all worries and thoughts. You can visualize these thoughts as balloons filled with helium and watch as you release them into the air if you would like.
- Start visualizing your goal, just like your goal has been accomplished.
- Feel the feelings that you will feel if you had already accomplished your goals. You might feel relieved, relaxed, and happy. Visualize what your life would be like if you had accomplished these goals.
- Once you have a clear vision, say your chant over and over until you feel the energy being raised. Once you feel your goal is about to burst out of your mind, light the candle.
- Visualize the aura around the candle is getting larger and filling the room. Watch as it grows larger and expands out into the Universe. You can continue saying your spell if you would like.
- Take as much time as you need to so you can imagine yourself getting your goal. Hold onto that vision as long as you can.

Candle Safety

Some spells might call for you to let the candle burn out completely. It isn't ever good to leave a burning candle unattended. If you have to, make sure you put it in a flameproof container away from anything flammable. Be careful when using anointing oils because they are very flammable, and you don't want ever to burn your fingers.

Be sure the candle is in a proper holder and let it burn out by itself. It might go out before it is finished, or it might totally melt into nothingness. Either way is perfectly fine. Never relight the candle.

When the candle is done, bury the remnants outside and know that your ritual is complete.

If you do candle magic by using the right precautions along with a direct and sincere focus and not meaning harm to any, you will soon see the success that will encourage you to keep exploring magic.

More on Candle Magic

More complex spells might include using the visualizations and charges over several days. If this is the case, you will blow out the candle every night and then relight it the next day once you are ready to continue your spell.

Other methods might use many candles; one represents the caster, one represents the target, and one or multiple candles will represent the goal.

All of it is just a part of candle magic's beauty. Suppose it is flexible so you can literally design your spell around your needs. You can keep it simple with only a few supplies. Just keep practicing to see how well you can grow your skills.

Casting Spells Specific to the Days of the Week

Magic doesn't just rely on the moon's phases or planets but on certain days to coordinate the candles' lighting.

- Sunday: optimism, general positive work, blessings, healing
- Monday: marriage, spiritual work, psychic work, fertility, childbirth, women's concerns
- Tuesday: health, strength, banishing, break ups, enemy work, war work
- Wednesday: gambling, faster results, negotiations, travel, business, communication
- Thursday: legal problems, business, money, success, wealth, power
- Friday: creativity, admiration, business, prosperity, beauty, sex, love
- Saturday: justice, revenge, creating structure, clarifying, blocking, binding, enemy work

Fixing Problems

Anytime you do candle magic, you are trying to shift something in your favor and make the candle do your bidding. The perfect flame for a candle is for it to burn with a medium-size flame. The flame shouldn't be too smoky and high but not too small that it stops burning. If the flame is burning too high, you can trim the wick to about one-quarter of an inch. If the flame is too low or goes out, you might need to pour off some wax so that the wick will be taller.

If you are working with more than one candle and burn them on several days, they need to burn at the same rate each day. If one candle burns faster, snuff the fast burning one out early so that the slow one can catch up.

Interpreting the Candle Wax

A great thing about using candles for magic is that you can

get feedback from the spirits as to what you can expect from the spell. A good way to do this is to look for smoke or soot on the glass, look for excess was, and reading the wax remains.

- For Candles Burned in Glass Holders

Black smoke or soot shows there are blockages around your intention. How much soot shows the blockage is heavy. You will need to redo the spell and begin by purifying the energy in the room and candle. Once the cleansing candle burns completely and cleanly, light a different candle for your intentions. You might want to make your magic stronger by doing some cleansing baths.

If you have white or grey smoke, it shows that your spirit guides are around you, and they are there to help you with your intention. The wax that is left at the bottom of the glass shows that there is more effort and work to be done in the material world to help support your outcome. If the wax burned totally, it shows that there isn't any more effort or work you need to do.

If the glass breaks, it shows that somebody is working against you to have a good outcome.

- Pillar Candles on a Tray or Plate

If the wax is spilling over the dish or tray, it shows that you are revealing too much about the situation. It is either too much emotion or information.

As the pillar burns, if the melted wax remains to stand, it shows blockages. Tall remains show there are large blockages; short ones will show there are small blockages. When you have wax, stay standing to show that there are many blockages, while only a few means there are only a few blockages. Remains that start off standing but fall over during the spell shows that blockages were overcome or removed during the spell.

Suppose your candle wick is drowning in wax before it completely burns, which shows that there is some material work that you need to do to help your outcome. If the wax burns out completely, it shows that there isn't any more work for you to do.

If the dish or tray breaks, it shows that somebody is working against your outcome.

If you have been working with figurine candles and you see any specific parts of the candle remaining, this is also a message. If the feet remain, you can interpret this as "you need to get your foot in the door" or "keep your feet on the ground." It could also mean you need to get a "better footing" in your situation.

- Divination

In certain magical circles, candles could be used for divination. The two common methods of using candles for divination are reading the way the candle burns and reading the wax after it has burned. This is sometimes called "ceromancy." It is great for people who can see visions in scrying bowls, crystal balls, clouds, etc. As you gaze at the melted wax, look for patterns or shapes that might suggest things that might be taking shape around your intentions. Which direction did the air push the wax while it melted? What is the "mood" or appearance of the wax?

To divine by how the candle burns, you have to pay attention to whether the candle's flame is burning tall or low, if there is more than one flame, or if it flickers. Two flames might mean that somebody from the spirit realm is helping you with your spell. The colors within the flame might tell you how effective your spell is, too. There isn't any true reasoning about what these signs mean. Some practitioners think that a candle that burns strong and tall shows that your wish is going to come true. If the flame is weak and low, it might indicate that there isn't a lot of spiritual energy in the room. If the wick is producing thick or black smoke, there is an opposition working against you. This might be coming from another person, unknown circumstances, or your unconscious mind. Others believe that the wick's quality and length could influence the way the candle burns as air vent can cause problems, too. Try to focus on your intent rather than the way the candle burns.

If you would like to divine by reading the wax, you will need to drop the melted wax into some cold water. The wax will harden instantly and will form a shape. Use this shape to get your answers, just like you are reading tea leaves.

When you are reading the wax, don't overthink things. You don't want to change the energy that you have already sent through the spell by trying too hard to get new information. You might have to work many spells before you get a sense of how the wax and flames are communicating with you.

Disposing of the Wax

If you worked with an invoking candle, you might want to keep it in a zip-top baggie and put it in an appropriate place like your bedroom if it was a love spell or in your office for a money spell until the spell comes to pass.

You could also bury it in a potted plant or on your property. You could also form the leftover wax into symbols like dollar signs or hearts and put these talismans into a mojo bag or on your altar. If you need to soften the wax a bit, you can use a hairdryer and then form it into any shape you would like, such as a poppet or baby.

If you have used a banishing or uncrossing candle, you might want to bury it away from your house like in a graveyard or leave it at a crossroads. Leave the remains of the spell in the middle of an intersection where two roads cross each other.

When your candle has burned totally, your spell is finished. It would be best to visualize what you have worked on and expect to receive positive results.

WHEN WILL I SEE RESULTS?

This all depends on the circumstances around the situation. If the situation is challenging, it might take longer to see any results. The best thing to do is to look for small signs like seeing specific symbols, seeing a certain number, seeing specific works, or hearing a specific song. You should be seeing these signs in about three days after you have completed your spell. Look for movement toward your goal in about three weeks. Look for the final outcome in about three months. If you don't see any of these signs within any of the time frames mentioned, then you need to go back and put more energy into your spell, use new strategies, choose a different candle or do more spiritual work with your situation.

Remember this: every disease can't be cured with just one dose of medicine. It might require multiple doses. The same goes for spiritual work.

CHAPTER 2
PICKING THE BEST CANDLES

You might have noticed that flames and fired normally accompany many prayers and rituals. Fire has always been a huge part of most ceremonies and traditions. Since ancient times, candles have been used to light their altars. You should never underestimate the spiritual and magical powers of candles. When you light a candle, it exerts magic and creates a spiritual environment. Candle spells and candle magic are powerful magic types that seem subtle but can have powerful implications.

CANDLES FOR CANDLE MAGIC AND SPELLS

Candles are important to most rituals and spells. Their colors and shapes are also important when doing Wiccan rituals, Voodoo, Witchcraft, and magic. The way you cleanse, dress, and charge them along with their colors and being able to create enough energy is critical to your magic and spells actually working.

DIFFERENT CANDLES AND WAYS TO USE THEM

Many different types of candles are specific for effects and functions, and each one has been assigned to a specific spell. Some types might include seven-day candles, zodiac candles, pillars, and shapes. Pillar candles are the most common and can be used daily. They come in various colors and are used because of their longevity. Each candle has a specific use. Chakra candles get used to cleanse our bodies and to provide holistic effects. The shaped ones are used for case-specific spells.

Jumbo, Pillar, and Altar

These candles are tall and thick. They burn slowly. This is why they are great to be used as deity or altar candles because they get lit first but extinguished last. These can also be found in glass containers as seven-day candles.

Scented Candles

You can use scented candles in your spells. Below you will find a list that shows you the magical properties of every scent:

- Patchouli: attracts money
- Vanilla: sexual passion, enhance memory
- Pine: getting rid of negative energies, strength
- Tangerine: prosperity
- Rose: love
- Strawberry: luck, friendship, love
- Myrrh: purification, protection
- Sandalwood: purification, healing, protection
- Blueberry: keeps negative energy away
- Musk: courage, strength, sexual passion, love
- Carnation: healing

- Lotus: inner peace, harmony
- Cherry: attracts love
- Jasmine: love
- Cinnamon: good fortune, attracts wealth
- Honeysuckle: psychic abilities, healing, good luck
- Coconut: protection, purification
- Frangipani: attracts positive energy

Crucifix or Cross

These candles can be used to banish spells or for protection. They are also very beneficial to be used as an offering to Lwa, a saint, God, deities, or Orisha.

Devil-Be-Gone and Satan

These are in the shape of the Christian's devil and can be used to remove spirits, negative energies, entities, and exorcisms. Burn it with an astral candle to represent someone who needs to be cleansed.

. . .

Seven-Knob

These candles consist of seven evenly sized knobs. You can burn one each day while you are focusing on your desires, goals, and wishes. Because it takes seven days to burn completely, it makes your magic extremely potent. The following will help you know what color to burn:

- Green: manifesting, court cases spells, money spells
- Blue: confusion, fights, stop depression
- Orange: getting rid of obstacles, success in business
- Purple: spiritual protection, defeating spiritual attacks
- Brown: justice spells
- White: granting secret wishes, purification
- Red: putting energy into motion, love spells, getting rid of obstacles
- Yellow: getting rid of bad luck
- Black: releasing spells, banishing spells

Skull and Mummy

Skull candles look like skulls, and mummy candles look like a mummy lying in a coffin. These candles offer protection and are great when warding off death, illness, and dangerous situations.

Cat

These will be in the shape of a cat, obviously. Use a black one to break jinxes, hexes and to break curses. They can be used to attract good luck and to get rid of bad luck. A green one can help with healing and prosperity, especially if you are trying to heal your pet. If you want to increase the potency of love spells, use a red one.

. . .

Eve and Adam

These are in the shape of a nude female and male. You can find them in many colors. They are used in attraction and love spells. You can use them to bring love to your life, bring back a lost love, push away unwanted love, or break up relationships.

Zodiac or Astral

These candles can represent another person or yourself in a ritual or spell. They have many uses and could be used in various rituals. Be sure that you never throw them away. It would be best if you always allowed them to burn out completely or store them safely. Use the color list below to help you pick the right one for your spells:

- Aries: red, pink, white
- Taurus: pink, green, yellow, red
- Gemini: silver, yellow, blue, red
- Cancer: white, brown, green
- Leo: orange, gold, green, red
- Virgo: yellow, grey, black, gold
- Libra: light brown, blue, black
- Scorpio: red, black, brown
- Sagittarius: purple, blue, red, gold
- Capricorn: black, brown, red
- Aquarius: green, blue
- Pisces: blue, green, white

Taper

These candles are thin and tall, and you have to be careful when dressing and anointing them. These are best when quick results are needed. Make sure you always use a holder, and be sure the ones you get are colored all the way through and not just on the outside.

Table

These candles can be found in most stores and can be used in most rituals. Try to find the best quality and be sure they haven't been dipped.

USING VARIOUS COLORS IN YOUR SPELLS

A candle's color plays an important role since every color brings its own energy and power. This is why it is important to choose the right color for the spell's purpose and intention. The following shows what every color symbolizes and stands for, along with their magical properties.

Violet

This is the color of power. Blue can increase your psychic awareness. Violet will increase your magical powers. Burn one with other colors to make your spells more potent. When you are casting a healing spell, burn a violet candle with a blue one; violet will strengthen your desire to cast a healing spell. It can be used in spells relating to increasing your spiritual connections, clairvoyance, confidence, and intuition.

White

This is the color of unity and purity. The color white contains every color. It has been associated with truth, spirituality, and illumination. White candles are frequently used in purification and defense rituals along with peace, success, and abundance spells. You can light them if you think you might come in contact with things that are unclean or dark temptations. White stands for power, innocence, and spiritual strength. It can also be used to forge connections with departed loved ones, getting rid of destructive energies, and contacting your spirit guides. If you aren't sure about what color you should use, always go for white.

Red

This is the color of health, vigor, passion, and energy. Red candles can be used to perform spells to bring back lost love, family relationships, friendships, self-love, and romantic love. This is the color of vitality and health. It strengthens and inflames the soul and protects against corrupt or negative influences. Red is the color of sexual prowess and passion. This color has been associated with Fire if you light a candle before a task that takes courage along with a heart that is steadfast like a first date or interview.

Yellow

This is the color of knowledge and discovery. It can improve your range of motion and imagination. This color has been associated with Air. If you light a yellow candle before you begin studying, it can help improve your recollection. It is very useful to a person who is serious about their magic. Shades of yellow could range from lime yellow, golden sunflower, and non-metallic yellow. It stands for charming, attraction, and cheerfulness. It can be used in rituals to make your dreams come true, such as getting your hands on the money.

Black

This is the color of absence or ending an existence. This doesn't mean it's bad. Black could help end bad things like bad luck, along with good luck. You can burn a black candle to help absorb the negative influences that are present. It is just like a black colored object can absorb all light. The color black can project strong appearances, especially in the magic world. It is great to use in repelling, reversing, banishing, and protecting against black magic. It can help remove negative energies and forces, create discord with your enemies, and break up spiritual blockages. It could be used in spells to bless the home, to help banish, and for ambition.

Pink

This is the color for connections. It represents communication and nurturing that is important to love, like a person's looks or magnetism. It can help bolster confidence. If you light a pink candle before your ceremony, it will emphasize the connection between people, like someone getting married. Pink candles represent romance, affection, and love and are used to cast spells for meaningful and long-lasting relationships.

Blue

This is the color of relaxation and happiness. It can promote healing and can strengthen your psychic link to the spiritual realm. It can be used for learning spells, solving problems, and communicating. If you don't sleep well, project a desire to sleep better into a blue candle that has been lit for a few moments before you get into bed. Make sure you extinguish it before you go to sleep. Blue candles can enhance your spiritual awareness. Use light blue instead of dark blue as they are more uplifting.

- Dark blue: these symbolize extensive and deep mental thoughts and true devotion toward spirituality. These

candles can be used for spells that are cast to make people moody or depressed.
- Medium blue: these will symbolize peace and spiritual fortitude.
- Light blue: these stands for calmness, perception, clarity in thinking, tranquility, and coolness.

Green

This is the color of luck, money, fortune, growth, and prosperity. It has been associated with healing. It is commonly associated with Earth. Light one before beginning a task involving money, like looking for a new job. Green is the color of harvest, financial and business success, money, and wealth. Use green candles when you are casting spells to achieve financial or business success.

Orange

This is the color of attention and energy. Burn it to attract objects or influences. Any spell that was designed to locate anything that was lost might call for using an orange candle. You can combine it with other colors to strengthen its powers. Orange stands for encouragement, thinking clearly, happiness, physical energy, and stimulating a positive mind. It can be used in spells for setting goals, creativity, and courage.

Gold

This isn't the same as yellow. Gold candles are used for solar connections, business endeavors, and financial gain. They can help with intuition, divination, great fortune, financial gains, and prosperity. Gold is great to attract healing, happiness, influence, money, and knowledge. Gold has been associated with the powers of the male deity.

Brown

This represents the natural world, particularly animals. You can combine this color with other colors to push your spells toward the natural world rather than yourself or others. Medium brown can pause actions and stands for being hesitant. Russet brown has some influences of red and stands for uncertainty in love and romance.

Silver

Silver is great to get rid of and dissolve all negativity and to emerge victoriously. It represents well that overtakes everything evil. It could be viewed as a different shade of white. Silver can be used for lunar connection, intuition, and reflection. Silver helps remove destructive forces and negative powers. It can neutralize negative situations. It helps develop psychic powers. Silver has been associated with the powers of the female deity.

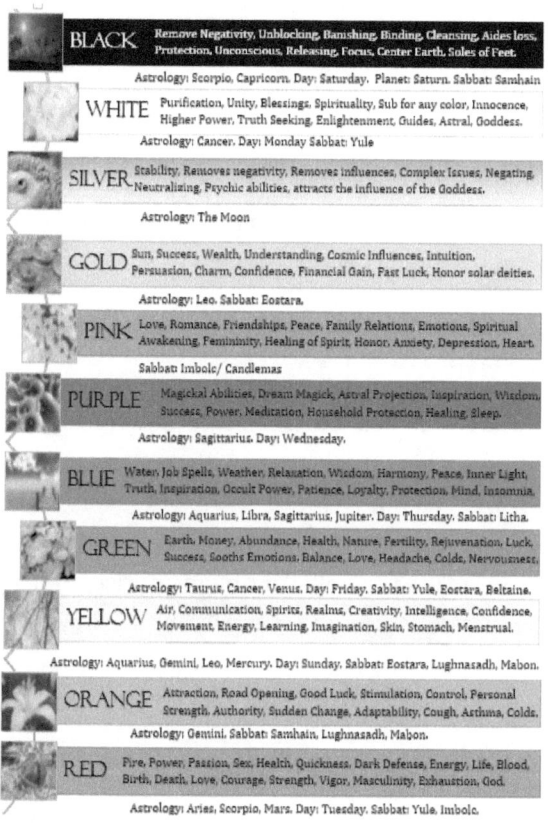

BLACK — Remove Negativity, Unblocking, Banishing, Binding, Cleansing, Aides loss, Protection, Unconscious, Releasing, Focus, Center Earth, Soles of Feet.
Astrology: Scorpio, Capricorn. Day: Saturday. Planet: Saturn. Sabbat: Samhain

WHITE — Purification, Unity, Blessings, Spirituality, Sub for any color, Innocence, Higher Power, Truth Seeking, Enlightenment, Guides, Astral, Goddess.
Astrology: Cancer. Day: Monday Sabbat: Yule

SILVER — Stability, Removes negativity, Removes influences, Complex Issues, Negating, Neutralizing, Psychic abilities, attracts the influence of the Goddess.
Astrology: The Moon

GOLD — Sun, Success, Wealth, Understanding, Cosmic Influences, Intuition, Persuasion, Charm, Confidence, Financial Gain, Fast Luck, Honor solar deities.
Astrology: Leo. Sabbat: Eostara.

PINK — Love, Romance, Friendships, Peace, Family Relations, Emotions, Spiritual Awakening, Femininity, Healing of Spirit, Honor, Anxiety, Depression, Heart.
Sabbat: Imbolc/ Candlemas

PURPLE — Magickal Abilities, Dream Magick, Astral Projection, Inspiration, Wisdom, Success, Power, Meditation, Household Protection, Healing, Sleep.
Astrology: Sagittarius. Day: Wednesday.

BLUE — Water, Job Spells, Weather, Relaxation, Wisdom, Harmony, Peace, Inner Light, Truth, Inspiration, Occult Power, Patience, Loyalty, Protection, Mind, Insomnia.
Astrology: Aquarius, Libra, Sagittarius, Jupiter. Day: Thursday. Sabbat: Litha.

GREEN — Earth, Money, Abundance, Health, Nature, Fertility, Rejuvenation, Luck, Success, Sooths Emotions, Balance, Love, Headache, Colds, Nervousness.
Astrology: Taurus, Cancer, Venus. Day: Friday. Sabbat: Yule, Eostara, Beltaine.

YELLOW — Air, Communication, Spirits, Realms, Creativity, Intelligence, Confidence, Movement, Energy, Learning, Imagination, Skin, Stomach, Menstrual.
Astrology: Aquarius, Gemini, Leo, Mercury. Day: Sunday. Sabbat: Eostara, Lughnasadh, Mabon.

ORANGE — Attraction, Road Opening, Good Luck, Stimulation, Control, Personal Strength, Authority, Sudden Change, Adaptability, Cough, Asthma, Colds.
Astrology: Gemini. Sabbat: Samhain, Lughnasadh, Mabon.

RED — Fire, Power, Passion, Sex, Health, Quickness, Dark Defense, Energy, Life, Blood, Birth, Death, Love, Courage, Strength, Vigor, Masculinity, Exhaustion, God.
Astrology: Aries, Scorpio, Mars. Day: Tuesday. Sabbat: Yule, Imbolc.

CLEANSING YOUR CANDLES

It would be best if you cleansed your candles to get rid of all energies that might have been infused in the candle while it was being manufactured, while on a shelf of a store, after being burned in a different room burned for a different purpose. You would need to cleanse all your candles if you didn't make them yourself while infusing them with a specific spell. Here are some ways you can cleanse your candle:

- Put the candle outside or on a windowsill where it will be in direct moonlight overnight.

- Make a bowl of sea salt and bury the candle in it for 24 hours.
- Burn sage or incense and hold the candle in the smoke.
- Saturate a cotton ball in rubbing alcohol and rub it over the surface of the candle. Move it from bottom to top to expel its energy.

MAKING YOUR OWN CANDLES

Because we are Witches, our spells are powered by our energy and intentions while interacting with our materials and the Universe. If you can pour a lot of energy into your tools, you will be making your spells more powerful. This is why you should use tools that you make yourself. You might notice your intentions will manifest faster when you power your spells with the tools that you have created.

Material List

You should do some research because there are pros and cons to every material. Choose supplies that are in your price range, and you are comfortable using. Above all else, listen to your intuition.

- Candle Wax

You can pick many options; the most popular are paraffin wax, soy wax, and beeswax. Let's take a closer look at each of these:

- Paraffin Wax

This is the most popular wax because it is readily available at most craft stores, and it is the least expensive. It is durable and can be used in any type of mold. The downside is this wax burns quickly. It is made from petroleum oil, and some say that it lets off harmful chemicals when burned. Some people say this wax is fine to use as long as you open a window or turn on an exhaust fan. Remember to do your research.

- Soy Wax

This is in the medium price range. It lasts longer than paraffin wax. This is a natural wax and will hold scents well. It will work best when poured into heat-safe containers or jars. Soy is more brittle than other waxes, so it is hard to use this for pillars or other molds.

- Beeswax

This wax will burn the longest, and it is all-natural. It does have a slight "honey" odor, so just remember this when adding essential oils. The downside is that this is the most expensive of the three.

- Molds

Instead of pouring your wax into a jar, you can use a normal candle mold. You could buy specialty ones from metaphysical shops. If you can find molds to any of the shapes mentioned above would be great for your spells.

- Wooden Dowels

You can use these to center your wick and poke holes in the middle of your candle while drying to make sure there aren't any hollow areas in the finished candle.

- Jars

Mason jars are perfect for making candles since they are heatproof and are relatively inexpensive. You could also buy metal, ceramic, or glass containers. Make sure whatever you choose is heatproof. It might be tempting to use old vases or cute glasses, but this is a huge safety hazard.

- Candle Thermometer

Use this to keep track of the temperature of the wax while you are heating or cooling the wax. Different waxes will have different heating instructions. Make sure you follow the instructions that come with your wax.

- Wicks

The most popular options for wicks are wood and cotton wicks. Both are available at craft stores or online and are fairly cheap. You will need to soak the cotton wicks in wax or essential oil before making your candles. You don't have to do anything to the wood wicks. These make a fun little crackling sound while they burn. You will need to get some metal wick holders and wick adhesive to place the wick in the bottom of the jar or mold. Read the instructions before to make sure you have to correct the wick for the size of your candle.

- Heat Proof Spoon

You use this to stir your wax. Please make sure they are heatproof, so the wax doesn't melt it. Finding one at a thrift store would be great as you won't ever be able to get all the wax off of it once it has been used.

- Double Boiler

While you are at the thrift store, see if you can find a used double boiler. You aren't going to be able to use it for anything else once you have melted wax in it. Don't spend too much money on this one.

SETTING YOUR INTENTION

You need to know what your plan is for your candles before you begin making them. Your intentions might affect what oils and herbs you use, the energy you conjure, and the candle's color while you are making them. You can make an entire batch of candles with the same magical intentions so you can save time on cleansing.

CLEANSING ALL THE MATERIALS

When you have gathered all your materials, you are going to need to cleanse them before you start making candles. Just like any magical tools you buy, your candle supplies are going to be loaded with random energy from all the people who have touched them in the store.

Since you will have a lot of supplies, using smoke to cleanse all of them at one time is easiest. Just light an incense stick or some sage and pass the smoke over all your materials. White sage, cedar, and sandalwood, incense sticks are great for cleansing. If this doesn't work for you, try to cleanse your materials out in the sun.

This is easily done by placing your materials in direct sunlight for a few hours. This method is great because the sun will infuse the materials with the sun's fiery, bright energy, and your candles will have the same energy.

COLORING YOUR CANDLES

Once you have melted your wax per the instructions, you can add colors. It would be best to use colored soy chips that you find in craft stores or online. It is the best option to give your candles vibrant, gorgeous colors.

Liquid candle dye is another option. These don't give you the bright colors that the soy chips will. Keep in mind that the melted wax is going to look lighter after it has dried. It is hard to know how dark the color will be until after it has set up for a few hours.

Don't use food coloring since these won't blend right with wax. Don't use melted crayons either. The crayon wax will clog the wick, and this makes your candle unusable.

SCENTING YOUR CANDLES

Most recipes tell you to add your scents just before you pour the wax into the jar or mold. This will keep the scents strong. You can use candle fragrances found online or in craft stores or use essential oils. Essential oils would be best since it is natural and are used by most Witches in the spells.

The downside is this can get relatively expensive, especially when adding them to your candles. It will take 100 drops of essential oil for every pound of wax to make a candle smell.

When making candles, it isn't important to have your candle a specific smell. If you know what oil will help support your spells, that is all that matters. If you know you are going to do a love spell, you don't need to worry about making the candle smell like rose oil. Just know that you have put enough in the candle to support the spell.

ADDING MAGICAL OBJECTS TO YOUR CANDLES

Try experimenting by adding objects to your candles while the wax is drying, such as old earrings or coins for abundance spell candles. You can add dried leaves or powdered herbs that go along with your intention for the candle. Take the tea out of a jasmine tea bag for dream and love spell candles. If you have any small gems or crystal pieces that you want to add to your candle, you can add those, too.

If the wax isn't cooled off enough, most of these items will just go straight to the bottom. If you realize this is happening, wait for about ten minutes and try again. As the candles cool, you will be able to distribute your items in the candle evenly.

Be sure you understand how each object will react to flame and heat. Don't ever leave a lit candle unattended, especially if there are herbs in the candle. You don't have to put a lot of herbs in your candle, just enough to make the magic happen. Be careful if you add these to your candles.

IMAGINE YOUR INTENT

Start your spell while you are in the candle making process by beginning your intention while you are melting your wax. While you are waiting for your wax to melt completely, imagine the outcome you want for this candle. This will add a lot of power to your candle since it could take about 30 minutes to melt two pounds of wax. This is enough time to get a very detailed vision.

DRAW SYMBOLS WHILE STIRRING THE WAX

You will need to stir the wax often while it is melting. You can use your spoon to write out words while the wax is melting that will support your intention. Writing phrases such as "abundance" or "new job" will charge the wax if you plan on using it for a money candle. You could draw dollar signs or sigil that hold special meanings to you.

WHITE LIGHT MEDITATION

It takes a lot of time when making candles, and there is a lot of waiting involved. You can perform white light meditation while waiting for the candles to harden enough to add crystal, glitter, or herbs. To perform this meditation, just hold your hands over the drying candles and visualize a white light floating down, coming through the crown chakra, and out from your fingertips where it goes into our candle wax.

USING MOON PHASES TO POWER YOUR CANDLES

The full and new moon phases are very powerful. Any candle that you make during these phases will have the maximum manifesting power. If you would like to make candles on other days of the month, think about your intention and the moon's energy. You might want to set an intention "to grow" or "to attract" for candles you make while the moon is waxing. Candles that are made during the waning moon could be charged to "release" or "banish" intentions.

TYPES OF MAGICAL CANDLES

- Tea Lights

If you don't have the time to make a batch of large candles, take some tea lights, put them on a foil-lined baking sheet, and place them in a warm oven until their tops start to soften. Take them out and sprinkle on some crystal bits, glitter, oils, or herbs. Use these for your quick spells. Glitter adds fun shapes to the wax while it burns. You can try to read the glitter puddles once the spell is over to find hidden messages.

- Knotted Wick

Take a cotton wick and tie seven knots that are spaced evenly on the wick. Set your intention and charge your wick with that intention while tying every knot. Attach the wick to the container or mold just like normal and add the wax.

Burn this candle for seven days; extinguish the candle when it burns to the next knot. By the end of the seventh day, your spell will be completed.

- Two-Tone Center

You can make the outer ring of your candle a different color from the color inside. This candle could be used for a dual intention spell or to reverse a spell. To make this, use a candle mold to create the inside of the candle. Once the wax has completely hardened, put this one into a jar or larger mold and pour in a different color wax that will fill the space between the wax and container.

- Multi-colored Layers

You can easily make a candle with different colored layers by pouring one color into your candle mold and then waiting about an hour for it to harden. Then pour the next color in and let it harden. These candles can hold different intentions to go together. You might want to put blue was on top of a "relationship" candle to help you communicate better with your partner. The bottom will be a red way to strengthen love and cultivate passion.

You could also use layers to represent the days of the spell.

You could even make a candle with seven layers for a week-long spell.

THINGS TO REMEMBER

- A good way to regain your focus is to look into the candle's flame.
- Meditate for some time, focus your wishes, and clear your thoughts, then begin your ritual.
- Using candles that you have made yourself will increase their power and potency.
- You can use any candle you would like, but beeswax ones are more powerful and burn longer.
- If your flame goes out while you are working your spell, this is a message. Pay attention.
- Try building a psychic link with your candle to bring more energy. Using the right oils can help.
- If you don't have a specific color of candle, just use white.
- Choose the right color for your intention. Check the lists above to pick the right one.
- Make sure protection is your top priority. Don't allow candle magic to catch your house on fire.

CHAPTER 3
TIMING SPELLS

Since the moment fire was discovered, it has played an important role in the spirituality of humans. There are also many misconceptions about candles, such as them being negative, but burning candles plays a big role in every religion in the world.

Candle magic tends to be intricate, and there are certain days that it is best to perform certain candle magic. There are also periods during the moon's phases that are better for certain intentions. This is just like how the color of the candle can repel or attract certain energies. Let's take the time to look at the best times to work candle magic to make sure that you attract the things you want.

DAYS OF THE WEEK

Throughout human history, the heavens have played a large part in our spirituality. The planets were all named after Roman gods, and these gods had the Greek counterparts that they were based off. Then these planetary bodies became associated with each day of the week. There is also a color that represents the characteristics of each of the planets. To invoke this spiritual energy, people can burn the candles in the correct color that is connected with their intention

Sunday

Sunday is the day of the Sun. This is the best day to do a spell that is meant to banish negative energies. It is also a good time to attract healing energies. The colors that are most closely associated with Sunday are white, orange, and yellow. The candles can be anointed with sage or lavender oil.

Monday

Monday is the day of the Moon. The moon holds the feminine spirit, and that is why this is a great day for intentions that involve communication. If you have an intention for reconciliation, it is best to do it on Mondays. The colors connected to Monday are the moon's colors, like grey and white. You can use lavender and ylang-ylang oil to anoint the candles.

Tuesday

Tuesday is ruled by Mars, who is the Roman god of war. Any intentions that have to do with courage or wanting loved ones to come home safely are good ones to do on Tuesdays. It also represents physical challenges and having the courage to face struggles in life. The color of the candle you should use on Tuesdays can be any shade of red. Clove and ginger oil are great for anointing your candles.

. . .

Wednesday

Mercury, who was the messenger for the Roman gods, is the ruler of this day. This is why this is a great day to do a spell that deals with business transactions, communication, and pursuing knowledge. You should think about using candles that are grey, purple, or yellow. Patchouli or frankincense oils are best used.

Thursday

Jupiter rules this day. This is a good day to attract wealth and luck. This makes it a great day to do magic that deals with attracting energies that heal. Farmers should think about burning candles on Thursdays with the intention of having plentiful and healthy crops. Candles that are brown or blue are best, and they should be anointed with lemongrass or rosemary oil.

Friday

This day is controlled by Venus, who is the Roman goddess of sex and love. This makes Friday a great day for performing spells that deal with love, partnerships, and relationships. Pink candles are best used on Fridays. Ylang-ylang is the best oil to use for anointing your candles.

Saturday

Saturn rules this day. This is a great day to work on intentions that have to do with major life changes. It is a great day to work on psychic wisdom and learning how to communicate with spirits. Intentions for finding lost items need to be done on Saturdays as well. The candle's purple, blue, black, or grey, are best. Frankincense or sandalwood oil are best for anointing your candles.

THE PHASES OF THE MOON

The Moon has the power to influence energies that can end up changing our lives. As such, it has the power to affect the spells we do. While doing a spell during the "wrong" phase won't hurt the outcome, timing it correctly can boost power.

The New Moon, sometimes called the Dark Moon, is the first phase. This is when it is the closest to the sun at this point. The only time we can see the moon during this phase is if we get its silhouette during an eclipse. So how do the New Moon and Full Moon affect our candle spells? Let's find out.

The moon is growing larger in size during the waxing moon while moving from the new phase to the full phase. This makes this the best time to perform spells that has to do with attraction. If you want to get a new job, attract more money, or find love, you should do spells for these at this time. This is a time for growth and adding things to your life.

The moon is shrinking in size during the waning moon and moving from the full phase to the new phase. During this time, you should do spells that deal with removal or getting rid of things. If you want to stop something from happening, you should do your spell at this time. This is also a good time to do spells that deal with protection. This is a time that deals with getting rid of things or decreasing the effects of something.

When the moon is new or at its darkest, you should set new

goals and new projects. Doing candle magic during this phase can help you start over while also providing you a fresh outlook on life.

After the moon has made a full journey, it is going to be full once more. At this time, you should celebrate everything you have accomplished. You should make sure that you are grateful for everything you have and have accomplished this month. The magic that has to deal with increased psychic ability, self-improvement, and motivation is best done during the full moon.

The power that candle magic holds is beyond what most humans can comprehend. We understand that certain days and certain moon phases can improve our spells and bring the things we want to us faster. That's why we are going to go over the best ways to prepare a spell for the best time.

GETTING YOUR SPELL PREPARED

The first thing you will need to do is to pick out a color that represents the outcome you want. You will want to carve your astrological symbol and name into the candle. You can also choose to carve sigils or runes into your candle at this time as well. Depending on your candle's size, you can also draw a picture or write out a word. Before you set your candle up in its holder, you can also place an offering underneath the candle that it will sit on. These offerings could be an herb or even some honey. You can also fill the carvings you make on your candle with glitter; just make sure that color matches up.

. . .

If you are using a pillar candle inside a glass holder and can't be removed, you can decorate the outside of the glass container. You can easily print off pictures, use some old greeting cards, or cut pictures out of old magazines and glue them onto the glass. You can create a collage on the glass as well. To make it look a bit rustic, you can tear or burn the edges of the pictures. You could also write the spell on a piece of parchment paper and then glue it onto the holder. You will want to make sure that the images are placed underneath the top rim and on the outside to catch on fire.

Before you light the candle, you need to make sure that you cleanse yourself by taking a bath in some Epsom salts. During this time, make sure you are focused on your intention. Once your body and mind are ready, take the time to meditate and visualize your intention coming to you, and then you can light the candle. If you do need to extinguish the candle before you let it burn out completely, that is fine. Make sure that you relight the candle once you are ready; just remember to follow the same steps of cleansing, grounding, and so on.

WORKING WITH THE FULL MOON

The Full Moon's influence can be felt three days before and three days after the actual Full Moon. Take this time to do any magic that has to do with success, gain, completion, and accomplishment. This is also the best time to anoint and bless your tools. If you have a spell that calls for more than one herb, oil, or color, you can use them all effectively.

Full Moon Items for **Strength**:

- Herbs: Thistle, St. John's Wort, Saffron
- Oils: Pine, Patchouli, Cedar
- Planets: Mars, Sun
- Candle Colors: Gold, Orange, Red

Full Moon Items for **Purification**:

- Herbs: Lemon Verbena, Cedar, Anise
- Oils: Olive, Myrrh, Frankincense
- Planets: Sun, Saturn
- Candle Colors: White, Black, Rainbow

Full Moon Items for **Peace**:

- Herbs: myrtle, morning glory, cedar, anise
- Oils: tuberose, magnolia, benzoin
- Planets: Venus, Jupiter, Saturn
- Candle Colors: pink, black, white

Full Moon Items for **Love**:

- Herbs: moonwort, cardamom, basil
- Oils: rose, clove, jasmine
- Planets: Moon, Pluto, Mars, Venus
- Candle Colors: red, green, pink

Full Moon Items for **Health**:

- Herbs: mullein, larkspur, coriander
- Oils: sandalwood, myrrh, eucalyptus, carnation
- Planets: Moon, Pluto, Mars, Venus
- Candle Colors: green, pink, light blue

Full Moon Items for **Friendship**:

- Herbs: passionflower, lemon
- Oils: sweet pea
- Planets: Moon, Venus, Jupiter
- Candle Colors: brown, pink, gold

Full Moon Items for **Energy**:

- Herbs: rosemary, pine
- Oils: citrus
- Planets: Mars, Sun
- Candle Colors: red, gold

Full Moon Items for **Employment:**

- Herbs: Devil's shoestring
- Oils: cinnamon
- Planets: Mercury, Jupiter, Sun
- Candle Colors: brown, orange

Full Moon Items for **Success**:

- Herbs: yarrow, vervain, fennel
- Oils: bay
- Planets: Saturn, Jupiter, Mercury, Saturn
- Candle Colors: green, orange, gold

Full Moon Items for **Manifesting**:

- Herbs: heather, mugwort
- Oils: heliotrope
- Planets: Jupiter, Sun, Uranus
- Candle Colors: orange, gold, red, green

Full Moon Items for **Happiness**:

- Herbs: lavender, rosemary
- Oils: sweet pea
- Planets: Jupiter, Venus, Sun
- Candle Colors: pink, yellow, gold

Full Moon Items for **Abundance**:

- Herbs: mustard, allspice
- Oils: cinnamon

- Planets: Jupiter
- Candle Colors: green

WORKING WITH THE NEW MOON

During this time, you need to focus on cleansing and banishing. This is also the best time for meditations and divination work. Whereas there were a lot of things you can work on during the Full Moon, there are three basic things that you should focus on during the New Moon.

New Moon Items for **Protection**:

- Herbs: nettle, mullein, rue
- Oils: patchouli, myrrh, cypress
- Planets: Neptune, Pluto, Saturn, Mars
- Candle Colors: grey, black, indigo

New Moon Items for Releasing **Negativity**:

- Herbs: rue, holly, fennel
- Oils: basil
- Planets: Pluto, Neptune, Moon, Saturn
- Candle Colors: purple, white, silver, black

New Moon Items for **Divination**:

- Herbs: cinqfoil, anise, mugwort

- Oils: sage, frankincense
- Planets: Mercury, Neptune, Uranus
- Candle Colors: yellow, lavender, gold

NEW AND FULL MOON MAGIC

Some things can be done in either the new or full moon.

Items for **Contacting Spirits**:

- Herbs: mace, dittany, orris root
- Oils: basil, frankincense, bay
- Planets: Mercury, Saturn, Neptune, Pluto
- Candle Colors: purple, indigo, black

Items for **Psychic Power**:

- Herbs: vervain, mugwort, mace
- Oil: sandalwood, heliotrope, anise
- Planets: Pluto, Moon, Neptune
- Candle Colors: white, black, purple

Items for **Meditation**:

- Herbs: chamomile, benzoin
- Oils: nutmeg, jasmine, hyacinth
- Planets: Pluto, Neptune, Moon
- Candle Colors: silver, white, indigo

Before you work with candles, make sure that you place them in a safe place and that you never leave a lit candle unattended. This is dangerous and can end up causing a fire.

CHAPTER 4
ANOINTING YOUR CANDLES

If you have ever purchased oil blends from a New Age or metaphysical shop, you already know how great these oils can be and how much they will be added to the spellwork you do. Luckily, there are a lot of places where you can purchase great oils like this all over the world. However, you must ignore the fact that you can create your own oil blends. Not only is making your own blends a great hands-on introduction to working with essential oils, but it can help you to add a personal touch to your magic work. It is also going to help save you some money.

. . .

Long before recorded history was a thing, healers, priests, and shamans would use scented oils in medicine, rituals, and magic. They would use oils in charms, tinctures, ointments, incense, and many other magical creations for just about anything. They created these oils by heating up fragrant plants, barks, flowers, leaves, and other scented items in a carrier oil that was created from sesame seeds, olives, and other sources. Some of the earliest known oils made were cinnamon, myrrh, and frankincense, which are still commonly used today.

Throughout the passing years, steam distillation other distillation practices have been discovered, which has allowed for oils to be extracted from a larger range of plants. With the abundance of interest in aromatherapy's healing properties today, there is now an unprecedented number of essential oils that anybody can buy. This is great for Wiccans who are looking to add oils to their practice.

Using Oils

Unlike many other types of spell working tools, oils tend to be a bit more supplemental than a requirement. Witches can use oil to anoint various tools like crystals, amulets, and even their own bodies. If you think about using oils to anoint your body, you will want to make sure that you are using ingredients that are safe for your skin and make sure that you aren't allergic to any of the ingredients. Clove and frankincense are two oils that will often cause some sort of skin irritation, especially if your skin is susceptible. Use these oils sparingly, and always make sure that they are diluted in a carrier oil more so than any other oil. Once the oils are applied to the body, it will help to bring the oils' energy into the person.

Those who like to create their own incense will often use oils, which is especially great for charm-making and candle magic. All things that are used in magic can be improved by using oils, whether you use one oil or a blend.

Any plant-derived oil will add a powerful punch to your spellwork and rituals for two reasons. First, they hold the energies of the plants that they were created from. Plants are living beings. They hold their own form of intelligence that works with nature. Plants also have their own magical properties, which will get concentrated whenever they are formed into oils.

The same can't be the same for synthetic oils, which may smell a lot like the real thing, but they lack the natural ingredients present in real oils. While many witches have likely used synthetic oils with success, most of them will tell you that using the real thing is always best.

The second is that oils also hold the power of scent, and their scent will affect the human mind. Everybody understands this intuitively because we all have our favorite scents that can make us feel happy or relaxed. We also have scents that will trigger memories. A blend of clove and lavender, for some reason, will often awaken something inside of a person that is beyond our typical sense of smell, and it places us in a different state of mind. It places us in an area where we are more connected to universal powers, which means we can direct all of those powers to achieve something. Botanical oils can give us directly connected to our natural world and the spiritual world.

If you can't get yourself into a certain state of mind for your intention, you don't get the results you wanted to get from your spellwork. This is why incense will often play a very big part of a person's magical work. The strongly scented smoke wafts throughout your scared area and will place you in a state of mind that is not worried, at least not at that moment, with all of the ordinary details of life.

It will provide you with the power that you need to focus on what's within, connecting you to your higher power, or anything else that helps you in your work. Scented oils will also provide you with another way to reach that inner focus. Then you have magical oils, which are a blend of oils that have been charged with a certain intent, and are the most potent oils that you can use.

Creating Your Own Oils

Depending on what your preferences may be, your blends can be simple or more complex. They could range from two or three oils up to ten or more. The amounts of each used will also vary. Some of the recipes will call for about seven to ten drops of a certain oil per ounce of your carrier oil, and then some will call for 20 drops. If you are a beginner with this sort of thing, it would be best if you kept things simple and stuck to low-volume blends until you get a better feel for how different oils work with one another.

. . .

While there are many commercial vendors out there, what people believe that making essential oil blends is hard to do is actually very simple.

To make blends, you will have to start by measuring out your carrier oil and placing it into your blending jar. You will typically use two tablespoons or one ounce of carrier oil. Carrier oils include safflower, almond, sunflower, jojoba, or grapeseed. Then you will add the essential oils, one at a time. You should do this slowly and enjoy their scents as you swirl them together. You will start to notice that you are creating a more complex scent, the more you blend. If you are making the blend for a certain spell and intention, you can also visualize that intent.

Oils blends should be stored in a dark-colored glass bottle away from heat or moisture. It is also a good idea to write the date it was made on a label as well as the blend. Ideally, you should use a blend within six months.

Herbal Infusions

There is another way you can make your own oil blends, and this is through infusions. These are different than the essential oil blends in that you are infusing the actual herb into a carrier oil. This will take a lot longer than the blends I will share with you later. These normally take about two to four weeks to make. Once you have finished your infusion, you will filter out the herbs, and then you can use the oil like you would any of the other blends.

To make an herb infusion, you will need:

- Labels
- Dried herbs – whichever you want to use
- An oil base – like sunflower or olive
- Cheesecloth
- A glass container to hold the finished oil
- An airtight glass container to make the infusion

In the airtight container, fill it about 1/3 of the way full with your chosen dried herbs. Add in your base oil, covering the herbs completely and bringing it nearly all the way to the top. Shake the jar a bit.

Label this jar with all of the ingredients you used and the date you made it. Close it up tightly and then store it in a cool dark place. Twice a day, shake the jar for about two to four weeks.

After a few weeks have passed, open the jar, place the cheesecloth over its top, and secure it in place with a rubber band. Carefully tip the jar over top of the other jar, or even a bowl to make things easier, and let all of the infused oil strain out. Once the majority of the oil has been strained out, take the cheesecloth off and wring it out along with the herbs.

Bottle up the oil and label and date it.

These types of infused oils can be used to cook with, which can be great if you are a kitchen witch. If you are planning on making these infusions, consider these tips:

1. Pick herbs that will complement the aroma or taste of your chosen base oil.

For example, if you want to use almond oil for your base, pick a sweet-smelling and floral herb instead of choosing strong culinary herbs. Some common bases include vegetable, almond, sunflower, olive, jojoba, and avocado oil for these types of infusions. The most common herbs used for this are wormwood, thyme, sage, rosemary, roses, peppers, mugwort, lavender, hawthorn, elderflower, calendula, and basil.

2. Focus on an intention while you are making your infusions.

When you plan on using these infusions for spiritual or magical purposes, make sure that you focus on your intention as you make the oils and each time you shake the jar.

3. Think about your timing.

The phases of the moon play an important part in making these oils. For example, if you are making a money oil for money magic, it should be made during a new or waxing moon and then bottle it during the next new or waxing moon.

Let's go over some other recipes for creating your own essential oil blends to help you out.

LOVE INFUSION

You Need:

- Lavender flowers
- Rose petals
- Nutmeg
- Sunflower oil
- Rosemary
- Narcissus petals
- Poppy petals

You Will Do:

1. Mix all of the herbs and spices together.
2. Take a glass jar and fill it a third of the way full with the herbs. Then take the sunflower oil and fill the jar almost full with the oil.
3. Screw the lid onto the jar and shake everything together for a bit.
4. Place the jar into a cool, dark place, shaking for a bit every day for a couple of weeks, up to a month.
5. After a month has passed, strain the oil into another jar, discarding the herbs. Label the jar with its name and date. Keep the jar in a cool, dry place.

ENERGY OIL

You Need:

- Allspice
- Lemon
- Ginger
- Olive oil

You Will Do:

1. Mix all of the herbs and spices together.
2. Take a glass jar and fill it a third of the way full with the herbs. Then take the olive oil and fill the jar almost full with the oil.
3. Screw the lid onto the jar and shake everything together for a bit.
4. Place the jar into a cool, dark place, shaking for a bit every day for a couple of weeks, up to a month.
5. After a month has passed, strain the oil into another jar, discarding the herbs. Label the jar with its name and date. Keep the jar in a cool, dry place.

ESSENTIAL OIL BLENDS

The following are recipes to make your own essential oil blends. These won't have to sit and be shaken like the previous blends, but since you have to buy all of the essential oils, they can be a bit more expensive to make. Like the other oil blends we have created, you can use these blends to anoint candles, crystals, talismans, tools, altars, and any other spell ingredient that you want.

Blending essential oils is simple, but it can be tricky the first few times you do it on your own. That's why I'm providing you recipes. These blends will provide you with amazing blends and will smell great. When you create your own blends, it will take a bit of experimentation to get the smell and everything just right.

AQUARIUS OIL

You Need:

- Patchouli oil, 1 drop
- Cypress oil, 1 drop
- Lavender oil, 5 drops
- Favorite carrier oil, 2 tbsp
- Jar for mixing
- Funnel
- Small blue or brown bottles with lids

You Will Do:

1. Add the carrier oil into the jar, and then add in your essential oils. Take a small, clean whisk, and mix all of the oils together, stirring in a clockwise direction.

2. Once everything is mixed, use the funnel to pour the blend into the small bottles.
3. Label and date your bottles and keep them stored in a dark, dry area.
4. Aquarians can wear this to improve their personal power.

ARIES OIL

You Need:

- Petitgrain oil, 1 drop
- Black pepper oil, 1 drop
- Ginger oil, 1 drop
- Frankincense oil, 2 drops
- Favorite carrier oil, 2 tbsp
- Jar for mixing
- Funnel
- Small blue or brown bottles with lids

You Will Do:

1. Add the carrier oil into the jar, and then add in your essential oils. Take a small, clean whisk, and mix all of the oils together, stirring in a clockwise direction.
2. Once everything is mixed, use the funnel to pour the blend into the small bottles.
3. Label and date your bottles and keep them stored in a dark, dry area.
4. Aries can wear this to improve their personal power.

CANCER OIL

You Need:

- Yarrow oil, 1 drop
- Chamomile oil, 1 drop
- Palmarosa oil, 4 drops
- Favorite carrier oil, 2 tbsp
- Jar for mixing
- Funnel
- Small blue or brown bottles with lids

You Will Do:

1. Add the carrier oil into the jar, and then add in your essential oils. Take a small, clean whisk, and mix all of the oils together, stirring in a clockwise direction.
2. Once everything is mixed, use the funnel to pour the blend into the small bottles.
3. Label and date your bottles and keep them stored in a dark, dry area.
4. Cancers can wear this to improve their personal power.

CAPRICORN OIL

You Need:

- Patchouli oil, 1 drop
- Cypress oil, 2 drops
- Vetivert oil, 3 drops
- Favorite carrier oil, 2 tbsp

- Jar for mixing
- Funnel
- Small blue or brown bottles with lids

You Will Do:

1. Add the carrier oil into the jar, and then add in your essential oils. Take a small, clean whisk, and mix all of the oils together, stirring in a clockwise direction.
2. Once everything is mixed, use the funnel to pour the blend into the small bottles.
3. Label and date your bottles and keep them stored in a dark, dry area.
4. Capricorns can wear this to improve their personal power.

GEMINI OIL

You Need:

- Sweet pea bouquet oil, 1 drop
- Lemongrass oil, 1 drop
- Peppermint oil, 1 drop
- Lavender oil, 4 drops
- Favorite carrier oil, 2 tbsp
- Jar for mixing
- Funnel
- Small blue or brown bottles with lids

You Will Do:

1. Add the carrier oil into the jar, and then add in your essential oils. Take a small, clean whisk, and mix all of the oils together, stirring in a clockwise direction.
2. Once everything is mixed, use the funnel to pour the blend into the small bottles.
3. Label and date your bottles and keep them stored in a dark, dry area.
4. Gemini's can wear this to improve their personal power.

LEO OIL

You Need:

- Lime oil, 1 drop
- Orange oil, 1 drop
- Petitgrain oil, 3 drops
- Favorite carrier oil, 2 tbsp
- Jar for mixing
- Funnel
- Small blue or brown bottles with lids

You Will Do:

1. Add the carrier oil into the jar, and then add in your essential oils. Take a small, clean whisk, and mix all of the oils together, stirring in a clockwise direction.
2. Once everything is mixed, use the funnel to pour the blend into the small bottles.
3. Label and date your bottles and keep them stored in a dark, dry area.
4. Leos can wear this to improve their personal power.

LIBRA OIL

You Need:

- Cardamom oil, 1 drop
- Rose oil, 1 drop
- Ylang-ylang oil, 2 drops
- Rose geranium oil, 4 drops
- Favorite carrier oil, 2 tbsp
- Jar for mixing
- Funnel
- Small blue or brown bottles with lids

You Will Do:

1. Add the carrier oil into the jar, and then add in your essential oils. Take a small, clean whisk, and mix all of the oils together, stirring in a clockwise direction.
2. Once everything is mixed, use the funnel to pour the blend into the small bottles.
3. Label and date your bottles and keep them stored in a dark, dry area.
4. Libras can wear this to improve their personal power.

PISCES OIL

You Need:

- Jasmine oil, 1 drop
- Sandalwood oil, 3 drops
- Ylang-ylang oil, 3 drops
- Favorite carrier oil, 2 tbsp

- Jar for mixing
- Funnel
- Small blue or brown bottles with lids

You Will Do:

1. Add the carrier oil into the jar, and then add in your essential oils. Take a small, clean whisk, and mix all of the oils together, stirring in a clockwise direction.
2. Once everything is mixed, use the funnel to pour the blend into the small bottles.
3. Label and date your bottles and keep them stored in a dark, dry area.
4. Pisces can wear this to improve their personal power.

SAGITTARIUS OIL

You Need:

- Clove oil, 1 drop
- Oakmoss bouquet oil, 2 drops
- Rosemary oil, 4 drops
- Favorite carrier oil, 2 tbsp
- Jar for mixing
- Funnel
- Small blue or brown bottles with lids

You Will Do:

1. Add the carrier oil into the jar, and then add in your

essential oils. Take a small, clean whisk, and mix all of the oils together, stirring in a clockwise direction.
2. Once everything is mixed, use the funnel to pour the blend into the small bottles.
3. Label and date your bottles and keep them stored in a dark, dry area.
4. Sagittarians can wear this to improve their personal power.

SCORPIO OIL

You Need:

- Black pepper oil, 1 drop
- Cardamom oil, 2 drops
- Pine oil, 3 drops
- Favorite carrier oil, 2 tbsp
- Jar for mixing
- Funnel
- Small blue or brown bottles with lids

You Will Do:

1. Add the carrier oil into the jar, and then add in your essential oils. Take a small, clean whisk, and mix all of the oils together, stirring in a clockwise direction.
2. Once everything is mixed, use the funnel to pour the blend into the small bottles.
3. Label and date your bottles and keep them stored in a dark, dry area.
4. Scorpios can wear this to improve their personal power.

TAURUS OIL

You Need:

- Ylang-ylang oil, 1 drop
- Cardamom oil, 2 drops
- Oakmoss bouquet, 4 drops
- Favorite carrier oil, 2 tbsp
- Jar for mixing
- Funnel
- Small blue or brown bottles with lids

You Will Do:

1. Add the carrier oil into the jar, and then add in your essential oils. Take a small, clean whisk, and mix all of the oils together, stirring in a clockwise direction.
2. Once everything is mixed, use the funnel to pour the blend into the small bottles.
3. Label and date your bottles and keep them stored in a dark, dry area.
4. Taurus can wear this to improve their personal power.

CHAPTER 5
PREPARING CANDLES

Before you start using your candles in different spells, you need to learn how to prepare them for your spells. You have learned how to cleanse them, and that's the first step of preparing your candles. The next steps include anointing them and inscribing. These steps aren't as complicated as some people make them out to be and add so much more power to your spell work. Now, not all spells will require anointing and inscribing your candles, but many wills.

If you were to be performing a love or attraction spell to find love or strengthen a relationship you already have, you would want a pink candle or red and inscribe it with love-based symbols. Once you inscribe it, you would bless or anoint the candle with a love or attraction oil.

The same is true for a wealth or prosperity spell and ritual. You would use a green candle and then inscribe symbols and words that represent wealth and prosperity on it and then anoint it with prosperity oils.

Inscribing Candles

The first thing you need to do, after cleansing the candle, is to inscribe the candle. It is easier to inscribe before you anoint because the candle won't be slippery with oils. You would use symbols, sigils, or words that represent whatever it is your spell or ritual is about.

For example, if a person is performing a love spell and wants to be loved by a person you know, you can carve their initials and your initials into the candle. You can also use other symbols that represent love if you want, like hearts or ancient love symbols.

Having something with a fine point to scratch across the surface is the best for inscribing. You can use a safety pin, a special scribing tool, and you can even use an athame. Once you have chosen the item, you want to inscribe with, dedicate it solely for that purpose and use it only for that.

The things that you can inscribe into your candle are endless. You can even come up with a sigil that represents your intention for your spell. To create a sigil, all you need to do is write out a sentence that is your intention, such as "I want to bring a passionate lover into my life." Then you would go through and strike out all of the vowels. This would give you "wnttbrngpssntlvrntlvrntmylf." You would then go through and get rid of repeating letters, which will bring you to "wntbrspslvmf." You would take those letters and smoosh them together however you see fit into a witchy looking symbol. There is no right or wrong way to draw a sigil.

Whenever you inscribe your candles, you want to visualize the outcome you want from your spell. It should be its own ritual. After you have inscribed your candle, you can then "dress" it if you want to.

Anointing Your Candle

Anointing the candles will help you to charge them properly. You need to anoint the candle with oils that correspond with your desired outcomes. There are even some spells that call for bodily fluids to anoint candles.

How to anoint your candle will sometimes vary between sources. In general, most people will hold their candle in one hand and then coat their first two fingers in the oil and draw a line from the top of the candle down to the middle. Some will do this all around the candle, and then they will turn the candle and do the same from the bottom to the center. This will cover the candle completely in the oil.

As you are anointing your candle, think about the outcome you want to get from your spell. People will normally anoint their candle in a certain direction, depending on the spell they are doing. For spells that help you attract something, you would anoint from top to middle and bottom to middle. If you are trying to send something away, then you would anoint from the center to the top and then center to bottom.

Some people will do a single stroke from the top to the bottom to attract things, and then from the bottom to the top to get rid of things. Some people refer to covering the entire candle in oil as consecrating. When they do this, they simply rub the oil all over the candle instead of worrying about doing it in a certain direction.

Despite the fact that there are conflicting methods for anointing a candle, you really can't go wrong with it as long as you have a strong intention.

After you have anointed your candle in oil, you can then anoint it in herbs as well. You don't have to do both. It is pretty much just a matter of preference. Again, make sure that they correspond with the purpose of your spell.

We are going to go over the oils and their purpose, but if you can't find some of the oils mentioned below for love spells, you can always use lavender or rose oil because they can be used for all love spells, even if they are meant to break people up. The only difference would be the direction you anoint them.

- Money – jasmine, vetiver, heliotrope, peppermint, honeysuckle, bergamot, cinnamon
- Strength – carnation
- Harmony – ylang-ylang, gardenia
- Protection - heliotrope, violet, juniper, rosemary, lilac, pine, patchouli, bayberry, myrrh, carnation, frankincense, dragon's blood
- Healing – frankincense, myrrh, carnation, lavender, clove, gardenia, cedar
- Prosperity – musk, bayberry

- Curse and Hex Removal – dragon's blood, yarrow, cedar, vetiver, myrrh
- Balance – magnolia
- Happiness – amber, gardenia, bergamot
- Purification and Cleansing – frankincense, cedar, sandalwood, dragon's blood, sage, patchouli, sandalwood
- Fertility – rose
- Control – bayberry
- Energy – peppermint, cinnamon, rosemary
- Creativity – peppermint, clove
- Dreams – jasmine
- Psychic Abilities and Divination – jasmine, yarrow, honeysuckle, myrrh
- Love: lavender and rose can be used for all
- Have someone fall in love – lavender, violet, jasmine, musk
- True love – ylang-ylang, rose
- Attract love – gardenia, amber, patchouli
- Lust and sex – orange, nutmeg, musk
- Break up – columbine
- Remove problems – Melissa
- Commitment – patchouli, rose
- Faithful – magnolia

If you want to use herbs and oils, you can use the same list for the herbs. All you would need to do is, once it is dressed, is roll the candle in the herbs. They will stick to the oils. When a candle is dressed, you will want to really watch it while it burns because it can pop and spark more than normal.

BASIC CANDLE SPELL

Here, we will go over seven simple steps that will introduce you to the world of candle magic.

1. Pick your supplies

Each candle magic spell will need a couple of things, to begin with, and obviously, a candle is the most important. The type of candle that you will pick will all depend on how you plan on using it. Glass pillar candles are pretty, but they aren't ideal if you want to carve things into it.

Besides making sure that your candle will work for your spell, picking one in the right color, scent, size, and shape are all important. Big candles might be fun, but they take quite a bit of time to burn out.

Other supplies that you may need include a way to light your candle, possible herbs and oils for dressing it, a holder, a carving tool, and any other items you need for your altar. You can also dim the lights or play some mood music if you would like to.

. . .

2. Get your space ready

The next thing you need to think about is your workspace. Remember, you are getting ready to work with fire, so you will want to make sure that your work is fireproof. Make sure you don't have any curtain nearby and that there is nothing on your altar that is flammable. Plus, watch out for children and pets. Singed whiskers won't give your spell a happy ending. You may also want to look at the type of clothes that you are wearing. Things that are long and flowy can easily end up catching fire. This is also true if you have long hair. Be safe and tie it back.

The way you set up your altar is completely up to you. Candles tend to d best if you place them front and center. You can add some pretty decorations that correspond with the season next to them as well. Placing all of the tools you may use to the right of your altar is useful if you are right-handed. You may want to place them on the left if you are left-handed. You can then place a little notebook on the opposite side.

Unless you plan on calling on a deity to help with your spell, this setup is not an altar for worship. It is simply a workspace altar that is simply meant to be useful. This is your workspace to use as you will, and you don't necessarily have to worry about being disrespectful.

3. Get your candle ready

Now would be the time to get your candle ready for your spell. This works in three steps. The first would be carving your candle. Take the pointy object you had dedicated for this process and carve whatever you feel led to carve into your candle, as long as it relates to your intention.

. . .

Then you will dress the candle with the oil. You have the list above of oils that relate to certain intentions, but you can also use plain olive oil if you need to. Once you have oiled the candle, you can then roll it into some herbs. Then you can set the candle in its respective holder and then go clean your hands because you will probably be covered in oils and herbs.

4. Light your candle

This is as simple as it sounds. All you have to do is light the candle. You can use matches or a lighter, whatever works for you.

5. Focus your mind on your intention as your candle burns

There are many different ways that you can do this. You can simply sit there and daydream or meditate about your intention. You can also chant if you think you can come up with a little chant that represents your intention. You also have the option of journaling, or you can say your intention out loud. It is up to you as to how you can do this; just try to find a way to focus all of your energy on what your spell's purpose is. This is the part where you are really pouring all of your energy into your spell and then charging the intention you have created for your spell, so you need to spend some time here.

6. Blow it out or let it burn

There is a big dispute about this in different Witch circles. Some people think that if you blow the candle out, you are "extinguishing" your intention and that you should allow the candle to burn completely out by itself. I don't think this is necessarily true. Your breath can sometimes be one of your most powerful tools. Blowing out your candle when you finish your spell can be viewed as a way to release your power into the world. You shouldn't be afraid to blow out your candle if you feel like you should.

There are times, though, where you will need to let your candle burn out completely. There will be a spell in this book that will tell you to let it burn out, and if you are making up your own spell, you should let it burn out if it has to do with banishing or other types of magic along those lines. But, make sure you never leave that candle unattended. You need to stay in the room with it for the entire time. You don't want to burn down your house as well.

7. Dispose of the remnants

Disposing of the remains of your spells is a personal decision. There are some who will throw things in their trash, and others will set things on fire. It is best not to bury or throw things in water unless they are biodegradable. If they aren't biodegradable, you are simply littering.

You can also keep your spell's remains and use them to reverse the spell if you find that you need to. You should make sure you properly label your spell remnants if you plan on using them for this reason. You don't want to end up undoing the wrong spells.

And that's it. These are the most basic steps to one of the most basic candle spells that you can do.

CHAPTER 6
CANDLES FOR ALL OCCASIONS

Purchasing candles is not hard in any way. Almost every store will carry some kind of candle. You probably already have your favorite places to purchase candles, but we are going to look at some of the best ways to make sure you have a large stock of candles so that you are prepared for any spell.

We've covered the meaning of the colors, and we've talked about the different sizes, so let's simply jump into how to create your collection.

The first thing you need to do is to make sure that you have candles of different sizes. The most common sizes you will need are chime, taper, votive, pillar, tealight, and jar.

Chime candles will burn for about two hours and tend to be the best choice for individual spells that only require a single burning session. These are probably the ones that you want to have the most of. You want to make sure that you always have at least two of each color in this size at all times. The colors that you should keep on hand are white, black, brown, silver, purple, blue, green, pink, red, orange, copper, silver, gold, and yellow. A great alternative to chime candles, and if you can't find anything else, are birthday candles. They burn quickly, so it is great for quick spells where you can babysit the candle when you need it to burn out completely.

Chime candles aren't as common in stores, and you would have better luck at finding them online. Some great places to find a variety of packs of chime candles are Amazon and Etsy. You can often find a set of 20 chime candles, two candles of ten different colors for about $10. Finding them in copper, gold, or silver can be a problem at times, and you will probably pay more for them.

Going to metaphysical shops, either online or in-person, might help you find the best deals for chime candles, too. They will have a larger variety of colors. Sites like 13moons and Wicca.com are great options for stocking up on chime candles.

Then there is the taper candle. These take about 12 hours to burn, so if you have a spell that requires the candle to burn all the way out, make sure you have enough time to watch the candle until it has burned out. The 12-hour rule is only true for a 12-inch taper candle. The longer the candle is, the longer it takes to burn out. The tie to burn out is about one hour per inch. These are best used when you can snuff out the candle since they take so long to burn out. Or you could use these when you have to relight a candle for several days, as long as you know it will last for the entire time.

. . .

You don't really have to have a lot of these on hand, especially if you are a solitary practitioner, because you will use the chime candles more often. Again, try to have at least one in each color listed above if you want to use tapers.

Tapers can be bought just about anywhere. You can even find them at the Dollar Store if you are lucky. You can also buy them online, but they tend to be more expensive. You can also try to site yummicandles.com. You can get a set of 12 for as little as $15.

Next up are votive candles. Votives are typically about two-inches tall and around two inches in diameter. These candles easily stand up on their own, whereas the previous two will need to have a holder. A lot of companies claim that their votive candles will burn anywhere from 10 to 18 hours; the truth is that they only last about four hours. These are great when you know your spells are going to last for longer than three hours. They are also a great option for sealing larger witch's bottles. Having a few votives on hand in a variety of colors is a great idea. I would suggest having the same number of votives and chime candles because you will use them the most.

Votive candles tend to be some of the cheapest candles to buy, and you can find them anywhere. At Wal-Mart, you can buy them for 50 cents each. They also come in a variety of scents, which can help set the mood. Yankee Candle also has a variety of votives for just under $2 apiece. Online, you can go to yummi-candles.com and get a pack of 72 for $20. They say their votives last for 10 hours, but you will have to test that for yourself to see if it is true. You can even sometimes find packages of them. Again, finding them in the metallic colors of gold, silver, and copper can be hard. The great thing is, you don't necessarily have to have those colors because there is usually another color that will work just as well.

Then you have pillar candles. The three-inch pillar candle will burn for about 30 to 35 hours. The five-inch ones will burn for about 65 to 70 hours. The seven-inch ones will burn between 90 and 95 hours. These can either be used for multiple spells or for spells that require you to relight the same candle multiple times since they last so long.

You can also easily find these candles in most stores for a reasonable price and in several different colors. It is good to have a few pillar candles on hands in the most commonly used colors, like green, white, red, yellow, and pink. Michaels is a good place to find candles, especially pillar candles.

Next up, we have tealight candles. Most tealight candles burn for three to four hours, but you can find long burning candles that can last for six hours. These are fund candles to have on hand and can be dressed with oils or herbs, and you can even make your own rather easily. These are great candles to use for ritual baths. I would suggest having a lot of these candles on hand in as many colors as you can find.

The Dollar Store is a great place to buy tealights because you can usually find a pack of six or more for just a dollar. Going back to yummicandles.com, you can get a pack of 50 for $5. That means you are paying just ten cents per candle. Tealight candles are the best for the Witch on a budget because they are so inexpensive and they are versatile.

Last but not least are the jar candles. These are sometimes called novena candles. They typically burn for seven days, and they tend to be the safest candle to burn. These are typically used every day for seven days. One common way to use a seven-day candle is to focus on a different desire each time you let the candle burn. You set an intention, light the candle and let that layer burn down, and then snug out the candle. Repeat for the next six days, focusing on a new intention each day.

Some of these candles are also meant to help you align your chakras. It is up to you how to use these candles. Keeping a couple of these on hand is a great idea, but they are not necessarily a must-have. Chances are, you will decide you want to do a seven-day ritual. Many of these candles will have multiple colors in a single candle. You can typically find a jar candle in most stores for about $5, but they are more easily found online. You can also find h=them at the Dollar Store. You can also find them in most grocery stores in the ethnic food section if you don't mind them having pictures on them.

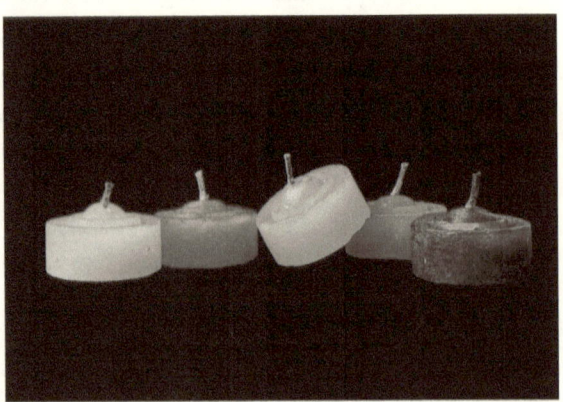

Now that we have gone over the candles and the best places to purchase them let's list out what you should typically try to keep on hand. They are ranked from the most to least important.

- **Tealight** – I suggest you keep a lot of these on hand since they are so versatile and cheap. You can easily have hundreds of them and not spend more than $10. They can be easily melted to add your own herbs and oils before burning them as well. Try to have as many different colors as possible, especially orange, white, purple, black, yellow, red, green, pink, and blue.

- **Chime/bell** – These are also a biggie for a Witch to keep on hand. They tend to be relatively inexpensive and can easily be found online or in any metaphysical shop. Keeping about two of each color listed above on hand is a good idea.

- **Votives** – These work a lot like the chime candles, so you probably don't need to have the same amount of both on hand. I would suggest choosing an either-or. Pick whichever one you like working with the best.

- **Pillar** – If you do a lot of rituals, these are great to have on hand. Having one for each Sabbat is a good idea. You can also try to keep one on hand for each Esbat as well. These are probably the best times to use these candles, especially for the solitary witch, since your individual spells aren't going to take that long to perform. Instead of trying to find pillars in every color, I would suggest just to keep this one in a simple white color. White can be used for any and all spells.

- **Jar** – Having maybe one or two of these on hand is fine. You don't necessarily have to have these on hand because they won't be used quite as often.

Now that you know the differences between the candles, you can begin creating your own collection. I have one final word on this matter, though. You should keep a lot of white candles on hand. White candles are extremely versatile and can be sued for any spell. If you always have a white candle on hand, you can do any spell that you want to.

Also, you want to make sure that you have a holder or dishes to place the candles in. You always want to be careful when you are using candles, and holders will keep the candle from falling over and catching something on fire. Chimes and tapers are the ones that definitely have to have holders because they won't stand up on their own. Tealights typically come in their own little metal holder. Seven-day candles are in a jar, so you don't have to worry about those. Votives and pillars should have a least a heat-proof plate under them to catch the wax. Some votives and pillars come in a jar as well. Just make sure you use common sense when using your candles so that nobody gets hurt.

CHAPTER 7
CANDLE SPELLS

This is what I'm sure all have been looking forward to. Here are all of the candle spells I told you about. Before we jump right in, I want to reiterate the importance of having a clear intention before you start any of these spells. You should never perform a spell "just because." You need a reason. Otherwise, you might get something that you can't handle.

SPIRIT GUIDE DREAM POTION

This spell is meant to help provide you with dreams from your spirit guides or any other power you would like to get guidance from. This should be done 30 to 60 minutes before you plan on going to sleep and make sure you have a journal next to your bed. This is great during the waning and new moon phases.

You need:

- Light or matches

- Water
- Athame or wand
- Graveyard dirt – you can also use dirt from a place that you feel a connection with, or you can omit this ingredient
- Lavender oil
- A cauldron
- Black tealight candle

You Will Do:

1. Add water to the cauldron that equals about a half of a cup. You don't have to measure it. You can eyeball it. Sprinkle the dirt inside and then say what your intention is. It works best if you come up with your own intention, but to give you an idea, you could say: "A bit of dirt to bring me closer to a world full of luster."
2. Stir some of the lavender oil into the water. Light the candle and put it underneath your cauldron. You will need to have your cauldron on a stand so that the candle simply sits under it so that the flame warms the bottom of the cauldron. You will start to smell the potion as it heats up. Let your muscles relax and allow your thoughts to start drifting around.
3. Sit with your cauldron until the candle has burned all the way out, the water evaporates, or you feel as if the spell is finished. Make sure you record any dreams that you have as you sleep that night.

BRING LOVE BACK SPELL

This spell is meant to reunite lovers.

You need:

- Red string or yarn
- Vanilla essential oil
- Pink, white, or red candle

You Will Do:

1. Using a sharp object, write your initials on your candle about half of the way down from the top. Then write your lover's initials over yours. This doesn't mean above, but actually, carve them over top of yours. Now, anoint your candle with some vanilla.
2. Tie the piece of string around your candle into a bow so that the bow is over top of the initials. Light your candle and allow it to burn until it reaches the initials. Gently blow the candle out and place it on your altar with the intention that you will finish burning it once your lover returns. Rub some of the oil over the initials each day until they come back to you.

HEAL A BROKEN RELATIONSHIP

This is a great spell to repair a problem in a relationship. This is great if you and your significant other have had a big fight. This spell won't fix differences between people, actually, but it can help them work through something that has happened to them.

. . .

You need:

- Ground dry basil
- White candle
- Thin lavender candle

You Will Do:

1. You will want to be patient with this spell because it can be tricky to put together. Crack the lavender candle in the middle but keep the wick intact. This crack represents the rift between you and another person that you are trying to fix. As you perform this spell, focus on this problem that you would like to overcome and how you could help to improve things between the two of you if you were given a chance.
2. Rub a bit of basil on the rough ends of the lavender candle's broken spot, then push them back together. Light the white candle and allow the wax to drip over the broken piece until the lavender candle has been mended back together.
3. Sit the lavender in a holder and light it. Let it burn until the flame gets close to where the break is. Now, sit with the candle and watch the flame as it burns through the joined break, thinking about different ways to improve your relationship. Once it has moved through the split, let the candle continue to burn out all on its own.

FIND HAPPINESS SPELL

You need:

- Dried lavender
- Two orange candles

You Will Do:

1. Place a couple of pinches of lavender on your altar between the candles. Light the candles and hold your hands up to them so that you can feel their warmth.
2. Say the following words seven times: "Please bless me with happiness." Allow the candle to burn all the way down, and you will notice that you are feeling happier again.

ABUNDANCE SPELL

You need:

- Large-denomination coin
- Vanilla essential oil
- Cinnamon essential oil
- Green candle

You Will Do:

1. With something sharp, write "Prosperity" up the side

of your candle and then anoint it with the vanilla and cinnamon oils. Place the coin inside of the holder and place the candle on top of it. Light your candle and allow it to sit and burn out completely.
2. Once the candle is completely burned out, leave the coin that is covered in wax in a safe place to bring more money into your life.

BRING PEACE SPELL

This is great when there is some lingering resentment that is preventing you from making up with a person.

You need:

- Yellow candle
- Small envelope
- Bay leaf

You Will Do:

1. Begin by writing your name out on one side of the envelope and the person you are upset with on the other side. Place the bay leaf into the envelope and seal it up. The light you candle and then place the envelope into the flamed. Place the enveloped in a heat-proof dish to let it completely burn. You can blow out the candle and know that your friendship will be renewed.

SPACE CLEANSING SPELL

You need:

- Salt
- Square piece of white paper
- Blue taper candle

You Will Do:

1. Place the piece of paper on your altar and place the candle in the middle of it. A clear glass holder is best to use for this, but if you don't have one, that's okay too. Sprinkle salt into a circle around the paper, making sure that all four corners are touching the salt.
2. When you reach the top of the hour, meaning 9:00 or 10:00, light the candle and allow it to burn all the way out whenever you can do this. Once the candle has burned out, carefully brush all of the salt onto that piece of paper and then swash it down the drain. Take the paper outside and bury it. The bad energy that was in that room will now be gone.

TWO PEAS IN A POD

This love spell is meant to help you find a similar person, somebody who has a lot of the same interests as you, or similar personality traits. Also, you may want to do this outside or close to an open window.

. . .

You need:

- Cup of water
- Lavender incense
- Rose essential oil
- Pink candle
- Real large feather

You Will Do:

1. Begin by anointing the candle with the oil and then light it. Light you incense as well. Start to think about the qualities you want in your significant other. As you do, wave the feather back and forth through the incense smoke. Catch the tip of the feather on fire with the candle and aim it towards the west.
2. Say: "Bring me my match; bring me, my mate, by this feather, I will not wait."
3. Take the feather and hold it close to your heart, it should still be smoldering, and say: "Smoke and air, come together with flair. Birds of a feather flock together."
4. Drop the remaining parts of the feather into the cup of water. Add a couple of drops of the rose oil and leave that cup on your altar. You will soon meet a person like yourself in some way or another.

MELDING LOVE CANDLE SPELL

This spell will help to bring you back in contact with an old loved one.

. . .

You need:

- Ginger essential oil
- Two red human figure candles

You Will Do:

1. If you are unable to find figure candles, two red candles will work just as well. Anoint each of the candles with some of the ginger oil and sit them next to each other in a heat-proof dish. You probably shouldn't use separate candleholders because you need the candles to touch for this spell to work.
2. Light the candles, and then start to think about the special loved one as the wax starts to run together between the two. Really concentrate on your loved one until the candles have become joined together by their melting wax. Then say the following: "Candles burn, and their waxes connect. We will once again be perfect."
3. Say these words several times until you feel that your point has been made. Then allow the candles to continue burning until they go out completely.

MORE CONFIDENCE SPELL

You need:

- Pure water
- White and pink rose petals
- Pink candle

You Will Do:

1. Natural water is the best water to use, but if you don't feel comfortable drinking rainwater, you can buy bottled spring water if you have your own well that is not hooked up to city water and isn't treated with anything that works as well. If you do have city water, you can use it, but it isn't ideal.
2. On your altar, form a ring out of the flower petals and set the candle in the middle of them. Before you light your candle, begin to think about your best traits and really concentrate on those things for a couple of minutes. Now, light your candle, and say: "Allow my light to grow as I learn how to glow."
3. Take a big drink of the water to clean out your negative beliefs about yourself. Let the candle burn out all on its own.

RED HOT LOVE SPELL

You need:

- Something with a point for carving
- Lavender essential oil
- Yarrow essential oil
- Rose essential oil
- Red string or yarn
- Three red taper candles

You Will Do:

1. Start out by carving a heart on each of the candles and then carve a pentacle inside each of the hearts. You don't have to do this perfectly; as long as you can tell what it is, it will be fine. Anoint each of the candles with one of the oils and then tie them together with the string or yarn so that the symbols are touching in the middle. Tie a bow into the string and then place them in a candle dish or holder.
2. As you light the three candles, say: "Live, life, love, I ask from above, three times three, bring them to me."
3. Allow all of the candles to burn a third of the way down, then blow them all out. Do this same thing for the following two nights until the candles have burned all the way out. You will start to see signs about somebody new entering your life for romance in the next few days.

REMOVE NEGATIVITY SPELL

You need:

- Dried sage, mint, or basil – you can also use all three
- Sandalwood oil
- Black candle

You Will Do:

1. Crush the herbs up into tiny pieces. Rub the oil over your candles. You want it to be slick with the oil and

then roll it in your herbs so that they are stuck to the candle. Place the candle into the holder and light it. There could be sparks because of the herbs and oil. Make sure that you burn it in a safe place.
2. As the candle burns, say: "I eject your negative thoughts. I eject your bad energy. I eject you ill spirit. I welcome peace and happiness."
3. Say this three times, and allow the candle to burn out completely. If there is wax that remains, bury it.

DREAM SEEING SPELL

You need:

- Large amethyst piece
- Black marker
- Small square of silver or purple fabric
- White candle

You Will Do:

1. With the marker, draw an eye onto the candle, the stone, and the fabric. Place everything onto your altar, and then light your candle.
2. Place the stone on top of the fabric so that their eyes are touching. Picture the eye in your forehead that can be opened up to see into all of your dreams. Hold this to your forehead, with eye touching your skin.
3. Watch the flame of the candle, saying, "open sight" over and over again. Place the fabric and stone back on the table and then allow the candle to burn out

completely. After you are finished, place the fabric under your pillow and sleep on it.

A NEW BEGINNING

You need:

- Rosemary oil
- Two white taper candles

You Will Do:

1. Anoint your candles with a bit of the oil and then place them in holders next to one another. Light one and talk about some of the old things that you have been trying to get rid of. Focus on these things for a few minutes and then use that candle to light the other. Blow out the first.
2. Now, start talking about some of the new things that you would like to bring into your life. Be optimistic when you do this, but also realistic. Let the candle burn until you are done. The first candle can be reused in a different spell if you would like.

PSYCHIC DREAM SPELL

You need:

- Sandalwood oil
- Dried mugwort
- Piece of amethyst
- 3-wick jar candle

You Will Do:

1. If you can find a lavender candle, that is great, but a regular white one will work just as well.
2. Focus on the question that you want to figure out the answer to while you are doing this spell. Sprinkle the mugwort over the candle's surface, and then anoint your amethyst with some of the oil. Tap the stone on your forehead three times to form a triangle. Ask your deity or the Universe to open the third eye.
3. Place the stone on the candle between the wicks. Place your hands over the top of the candle, and state your questions out loud. Light the candle and state the question again. Allow the candle to burn until it burns out all on its own.
4. Once you have finished the spell, notice your dreams for the next three days to see if there is anything unusual. Look for any recurring symbols or patterns that could answer your question.

FAMILY TOGETHERNESS SPELL

This is a great spell to do if there is a lot of tension in the house that has started to become a problem. It doesn't have to be done just on a family, but with any group that needs a little more happiness.

You need:

- Sandalwood incense

- Piece of clear quartz
- Handful of basil – fresh
- Pink candle
- Four candles of different colors

You Will Do:

1. This can be done on your altar, but it is best when you can do it in a central part of your home. Place the five candles in a circle. Place the quartz in the middle and cover it with the basil leaves—light your candles.
2. Light your incense and walk it through all of the main rooms in your home. Do this slowly and allow the smoke to really spread throughout. After you have done this, go back to the candles and sit the incense down. Allow everything to burn out on their own. You should notice that the tension starts to lift soon.

A BLESSED HOME SPELL

You need:

- A bell
- 3 copper pennies
- Rosemary incense
- Frankincense incense
- Sandalwood incense
- Three purple or blue candles

You Will Do:

1. Make sure your candle is big enough for a penny to fit in the holder underneath it. Place the candles in a triangle and place a penny in the holder underneath each candle in their holder.
2. Light one of the candles and then say, "I welcome hope," then light your sandalwood and ring the bell.
3. Light another candle and then say, "I welcome serenity," then light your frankincense incense and ring the bell
4. Light the remaining candle, saying, "I welcome good fortune," and light the last incense and ringing the bell one more time.
5. Place your incense burners inside of the candle triangle and allow everything to burn for a minimum, an hour. An entire afternoon is even better so that the energy of incense really gets to flowing through your home. Blow out your candles once you are done.

MOVING PROGRESS SPELL

This spell is meant to help you move along any issues that you may feel stuck on. This could be relationships, money, or anything else for that matter.

You need:

- Cinnamon incense
- Something sharp for inscribing
- Dark blue candle
- Pale blue candle
- White candle

You Will Do:

1. This will require that you look up runes to be able to inscribe them properly.
2. Start by carving the rune Thurisaz into the white candle in the middle. In the light blue candle, carve the raidho rune. In the last candle, carve the jera. Place each of the candles in their respective holder. The white candle should be placed to your left, the pale in the center, and the dark blue to your right.
3. With the cinnamon incense in your left hand, is to think about what it is that you want to work on. Light the incense and let the flame burn for a bit. Use this flame to light the white candle. Blow the incense out and place it in its holder. Say this: "This flame brings this spell to light. I need to take action instead of being trite."
4. Use the white candle to light the second candle, say: "This flame pushes the spell on. As of right now, the delay is gone."
5. Using the second candle, light the last one, and say: "This flame now brings this spell alive. Things will now begin to thrive."
6. Look at each of the candles and say all three statements from above, looking at their respective candles. Allow them to burn on your altar until they burn out. You should see immediate progress.

WINTER SOLSTICE RITUAL

You need:

- Red candle
- Small piece of white paper
- Mistletoe herb
- Hollyberry oil

You Will Do:

1. Start by writing a word in red ink on your piece of paper that represents what personal quality you would like to enhance yourself.
2. Sprinkle the mistletoe in the middle of the piece of paper and three drops of the holly berry oil. Twist-up the paper to close it with everything on the inside of the piece of paper.
3. Next, light the candle. Light the paper on fire with the candle. Sit it in a fireproof dish and picture what you wrote on the sheet of paper coming true. Once the paper is burned, you can blow out the candle or let it burn out.

FINANCIAL GAIN SPELL

You need:

- A piece of paper
- Several acorns
- Pine incense
- Patchouli incense
- A gold candle
- A green candle

You Will Do:

1. Carve the rune fehu into the bottom of each of the candles. Place them in candle holders that you sit across from one another. Place the patchouli incense next to the gold candle and the pin next to the green candle. Light the candles and start burning the incense.
2. Draw out another fehu on your piece of paper and place the acorns on it. If you aren't able to find acorns, you can simply use smooth stones. Allow the candles to burn out, and then leave the stones or acorns on your altar until you have extra money come into your life.

MONEY FLOW SPELL

This is a great beginner spell for anybody who needs a little extra cash but just can't figure out the best way to make it happen. This is also a great "starter" spell for people who are just starting out in magic. The trick to this spell is to quit trying to figure out how you are going to get the money because if you are just focused on how tells the Universe that you have no trust, it will work.

You need:

- Dried basil, a pinch
- A couple of drops of patchouli oil – olive oil can be used as well
- Crystal tip or pin
- Heat-proof dish or candle holder

- Green or gold candle – chime, tealight, or votive is best

You Will Do:

1. With the pin or crystal, carve a pentacle, or your favorite abundance symbol, into the middle of the candle. Then anoint your candle with the oil and roll it through the basil. Set the candle in its holder or on the heat-proof dish so that the symbol is facing you.
2. Spend a little bit of time centering and grounding yourself, and then bring up some feelings of excitement. This is the feeling you get when you unexpectedly receive money. Picture yourself standing in the middle of a flowing stream that is filled with money and coins. You should picture this in your countries currency. Once you feel that you are fully focused on this image, speak the following: "With this fire, I summon Nature's forces. Money now flows to me from hidden sources."
3. Now, light your candle. As soon as the wick catches, say, "So mote it be."
4. Allow the candle to stay in a safe place to burn all the way out.

CLEANSING SPELL

This is great if you feel if you have a spirit that is hanging around your house. This will help them to move on so that they stop bugging you.

You need:

- Sea salt
- White candle

You will do:

1. Place the salt in a bag or in your pocket because you will be walking around your house sprinkling the salt.
2. Take the candle in your right hand and then light it. Take a bit of the salt in your left hand. Do the opposite if you are left-handed. Then begin to walk back through your home and into every room. Sprinkle a touch of salt into the corner of every room as you loudly say, "Ghosts and Spirits leave this place and never return."
3. Once you are finished, travel to the northernmost point of your home and blow out your candle.

CANDLE DIVINATION

This can help you to get some answers about the future by providing you different signals as you are performing the spell. You will have to interpret those signals yourself because they will mean something different to everybody.

You need:

- Three candles that are the same

You will do:

1. Place the candles on your altars so that they are shaped like a triangle. Begin lighting them, starting at the top and then moving in a counterclockwise direction.
2. 2. Now, here are some interpretations of what you might see:
3. If you were to notice that one of the candles is burning brighter than the other two, then you can be sure that there is good fortune coming your way.
4. If you notice that one of the candles suddenly goes out, then you can expect a bit of negative energy coming into your life. It would be a good idea to do a protection spell.
5. If you notice that the flames are rising and falling a lot, be very cautious over the next couple of weeks because things are going to be a bit unpredictable.
6. If you notice that the candle flames twist and turn in and out of spirals, then you may have a close acquaintance or friend that is upset with you. You should also be wary of them because they can't be trusted.

FAST RESULTS SPELL

This is great if you are working on a project that seems to be taking forever to finish.

You need:

- White candle

- Slice of pound cake
- Glass of juice

You will do:

1. Take a moment to sit quietly and picture how it will feel once you have finished your task. Really picture this in your mind. Then call upon your chosen God or Goddess and say, "Please help me accomplish (insert task) quickly. For this favor, I kindly offer food and drink. Upon completion, I'll send you more. So mote it be."
2. Next, light your candle in honor of your chosen deity, and then state the task you need to finish once more. After your task is completely done, offer your deity more juice and cake to fulfill the promise you have made.

SIMPLE MONEY SPELL

You need:

- Oil
- White candle
- Green candle

You will do:

1. You can perform this spell at any time of the day, but

make sure that you keep the time the same for every day you do this.
2. The green candle is for money, and the white candle is you. Anoint both of the candles with some of the oil before you continue. As you do so, think of your desire for money coming to you. Place the candles on your altar so that they are nine inches apart. Once you have done this, say: "Money, money come to me. In abundance three times three, may I be enriched in the best of ways? Harming none on its way, this I accept, so mote it be. Bring me money three times three."
3. Do this spell once a day for nine days. Every day that you do this bring the white candle an inch closer to your green candle. After your candles are touching, the spell has been completed. It is important that you picture money pouring into your Universe.

REVERSING LOVE SPELL

This is a great spell to use if you realize that you have made a terrible mistake and you want to reverse a love spell you have previously cast. This should be performed during the waning moon for extra effect.

You need:

- White candle – chime is best
- Myrrh oil
- White silk clot

You will do:

1. Start by carving the name of your bewitched on the candle and then anoint it with the oil.
2. Light the candle and focus on your intention, and then say: "I burn this candle as a token of the spell that binds our love. Let this magic now be broken by the power of the Goddess above."
3. Let this candle burn completely out. Once the wax has cooled enough for you to handle it, wrap it up in a white silk cloth and then throw it into the river or another body of water you have easy access to.

CIRCLE OF LOVE SPELL

You need:

- 12 white or yellow candles – tealights or chime candles are best
- Rose oil
- Photo of you love
- African violet incense

This should be performed during the waxing phase of the moon.

What you will do:

1. Anoint the candle with the rose oil. Sit them in a circle that is big enough for you to sit comfortably in the middle of. If you want to, you can now call the corners as you normally would.
2. Sit the picture of your love, or who you want to be your love, in front of where you are sitting, and then

light the incense. Say: "As this circle of light surrounds (his/her) image so shall my love surround (his/her) heart as this fragrant incense burns with fire (his/her) burning desire for me shall start. (His/Her) love for me grows stronger as the 12 candles burn. As love is given, so shall it return. So mote it be."

3. Gaze at the picture and imagine a red beam of love-energy radiating from you to the photo as you focus on this visualization, chant or sing the name of the person you want to attract. Once the candles have burned down, anonymously mail the wicks to the other person.

DRAW YOUR LOVER NEAR

Before you perform this spell, make sure you know the kind of relationship you are looking to have.

You need:

- A green candle – pillar size would be best for all of the candles
- A white candle
- A brown candle
- A pink candle
- A red candle
- Large bowl – it should be able to hold all five candles
- For a woman – favorite lipstick
- For man – marker (or the woman's favorite lipstick if you know what it is)
- Oil – mistletoe, forget-me-not, iris/bay, lilac, or rose

You will do:

1. Begin by drawing a pentagram in the bottom of the bowl. For the women casting this spell, you would use your favorite lipstick. You can use a marker for the men casting this spell, but if you know the woman's favorite lipstick, then use it. Make sure you don't steal her lipstick, though. Buy a tube of it.
2. Place the candles inside of the bowl on each of the five points. Add pure water to the bowl so that it reaches halfway up on the candles. Then light the candles.
3. This is where knowing what type of relationship you want comes in handy. Red stands for passion, green for procreation, pink is for romantic love, brown is friendship, and white is for intellectual or spiritual.
4. Take five hairs from your head and twist them together and then let them melt into the candle that is the color of your desired relationship.
5. Now you need to add your oil. The oil will also depend on your desired relationship. Mistletoe represents procreation, forget-me-not is friendship, Iris or Bay is intellectual or spiritual, lilac is romance, and rose is passion.
6. Drop of few drops of your chosen oil into the water. Take your chosen candle and stir the water with it five times in a clockwise direction, putting the candle out as you do so. Then, carve your desired mate's name into the candle. If you don't know their name, write down the qualities that you want. Sit the candle, unlit, but you bed as you sleep. Each morning, light your candle and say this:
7. "Light of dawn, the light of thine, bring my lover's

heart to mine. May this day send them to me, to come in willing harmony. My heart to thine, forevermore entwine."

8. Do this each morning until you have a dream about the one that you want. You can expect the two of you to come together now. A different way to end this, if you want, is to contact your desired lover after you have the dream.

CONTACT A FRIEND

You need:

- Sea salt
- A cup of water
- Picture of person
- Sandalwood incense and oil
- White candle

You will do:

1. Begin by casting your circle as you normally would.
2. Then light your incense and anoint your candle with some of the oil.
3. Lay the picture of the old friend that you would like to have to get in touch with you on your altar. If you don't have a picture of them, write out their name on a piece of paper.
4. Take a bit of salt in your right hand and let it fall slowly into the water. As the salt goes into the way, say "contact me" repeatedly as you think about your friend contacting you. Sit the cup of

saltwater on your altar and let the candle burn out.
5. Leave the cup of water on your altar until it completely evaporates.
6. You should hear something from your friend before the water completely evaporates from your cup.

SAFE TRAVELS

You need:

- Sandalwood incense
- "personality" candle – make it a color that is appropriate for the recipient of your spell
- Photo or item for the recipient
- Purple candle anointed with sandalwood
- 2 white candles anointed with sandalwood

What you will do:

1. On your altar, make two rows. On the back, it should be all white candles, personality candles, and purple candles. On the front row, it should be a white candle, picture or object, and incense.
2. Start by lighting the white candles, then the personality candle, then the purple candle, and then the incense. Say the following invocation:
3. "Hail Mother of the world, see me, look upon me. See me, look upon me. See me, look upon me. Protect my people and me tonight. Send your white light around me. Send your protective light around (recipient's full name) as they travel and as they dream. Send only

good and lucid energies their way. Thank you. Thank you. Thank you."

4. Now you can choose to let the candles burn completely out now, or you can snuff them out in the reverse order to how they were lit. Then you can relight them each night if they are going to be on an extended trip. The last night of the trip, allow the candles to burn out on their own.

SPELL FOR SELF-ESTEEM

You need:

- Purple thread
- Jasmine oil
- Yellow candle
- Purple candle
- Lavender oil
- 7 green oak leaves – you can use bay as well
- A bath

You will do:

1. Start by running yourself a bath at a temperature that feels good to you.
2. Drop some lavender oil into the bath, and then add in the oak leaves. Swish the water around and light the candles.
3. Now, get into the bath. Close your eyes and allow yourself to relax. Start to breathe deeply. With every breath in, breathe in confidence. As you exhale, release your self-doubt.

4. Picture a yellow light glowing over your head that cascades over your body, touching every part of you. Continue to slowly breathe in through your nose and exhale through your mouth. Then, once you feel relaxed, say: "I am gorgeous. I am beautiful; I am Goddess." Say this six times.
5. Once you are finished with your bath, blow the candles out and then thread the leaves onto the purple thread. If you start feeling your self-esteem fail, heat some jasmine oil into an oil burner, light those candles, and hold the leaves up and say the chant again.
6. You can carry these leaves with you, either all the time or only when you have something important coming up.

HEALING SPELL

You need:

- Purple candle
- Black pen
- Fresh violets – complete with the stem in a vase or holder
- Scissors
- White string or yarn
- Purple paper

This can be done whenever you feel it is necessary, but it is best if done during the full moon.

. . .

You will do:

1. Begin by lighting the candle and fill a vase with some water. Place your violets in the vase and say some words that focus on the well-being of the person who is ailing and healing their illness.
2. With the purple paper, cut out a heart and write the name on one side of it and a little get well message on the opposite side. Poke a little hole into the top right side of the heart and place the white string through the hole. Tie this around the vase.
3. Give this vase as a present to the person to help them recover.

GET RID OF INTENSE EMOTIONS

This is a great spell to do if you need to calm yourself down when you have to face some intense emotions. This will help you to get through any stressful situations.

You need:

- Sea salt
- Bowl of purified water
- Black candle
- A pen
- Piece of unlined paper

You will do:

1. Start by lighting your candle, and then on the piece of

paper, start writing down your concerns, frustrations, and fears that you may be feeling.
2. Allow the words to flow freely. Don't try to hold them back. If you are moved to speak these words out loud, then do it.
3. After you have spilled your guts onto the paper, fold it up and then light it in the candle's flame. Once the paper has burned up, dip your fingers into the water and sprinkle some of the water on yourself as you say: "These words and thoughts and tension have left my life."

SPELL FOR LUCK AND PROSPERITY

You need:

- A piece of jade
- Gold candle

You will do:

1. Begin by lighting the gold candle.
2. Start to think about the changes that you would like to have happened.
3. Pick up the piece of jade and focus all of those changes into that stone. Picture all of the energy mixings with the jade and say: "Molding energies and Universal luck is coming my way. The door of fortune is opening, and starting today."
4. Picture the release of all of this energy into the Universe. Blow the candle and wear the stone on you to remind you to stay alert for any new opportunities

that may come your way.

SPELL FOR LUCK AND PROSPERITY

You need:

- A piece of jade
- Gold candle

You will do:

1. Begin by lighting the gold candle.
2. Start to think about the changes that you would like to have happened.
3. Pick up the piece of jade and focus all of those changes into that stone. Picture all of the energy mixings with the jade and say: "Molding energies and Universal luck is coming my way. The door of fortune is opening, and starting today."
4. Picture the release of all of this energy into the Universe. Blow the candle and wear the stone on you to remind you to stay alert for any new opportunities that may come your way.

ALL OVER HEALTH SPELL

You need:

- An orange candle
- A yellow candle
- A white candle

You will do:

1. Set the white candle in the middle of your altar. As you light the candle, say: "This candle is lit for a renewal of spirit."
2. Sit your yellow candle to the left of the white and say: "The flame of this candle brings imagination to me."
3. Sit the orange candle to the right of the white and say: "My body is full of health and strength."
4. Thank the candles for their help and then blow them out.

WINTER SOLSTICE RITUAL

You need:

- Red candle
- Small piece of white paper
- Mistletoe herb
- Hollyberry oil

You will do:

1. Start by writing a word in red ink on your piece of paper that represents what personal quality you would like to enhance yourself.
2. Sprinkle the mistletoe in the middle of the piece of paper and three drops of the holly berry oil. Twist-up the paper to close it with everything on the inside of the piece of paper.

3. Next, light the candle.
4. Light the paper on fire with the candle. Sit it in a fireproof dish and picture what you wrote on the sheet of paper coming true.
5. Once the paper is burned, you can blow out the candle or let it burn out.

WINTER PROSPERITY SPELL

You need:

- Myrrh oil
- Green candle
- Favorite Yule colored ribbon that is at least 12 inches long

You will do:

1. Start by anointing the myrrh oil onto the candle and then light it.
2. Take the ribbon and begin to tie nine knots into it. With each knot, recite the following:
3. "By the count of one, this spell has begun."
4. "By the count of two, prosperity is due."
5. "By the count of three, I'll have no more need."
6. "By the count of four, abundance galore."
7. "By the count of five, this spell is alive."
8. "By the count of six, prosperity's fixed."
9. "By the count of seven, blessings given."
10. "By the count of eight, I seal my fate."
11. "By the count of nine, praise the Goddess divine."

12. Wave the knotted ribbon through the smoke of the candle, not the flame, three times.
13. Place the ribbon someplace safe for the coming year.
14. Gaze upon it and meditate with it if you need extra strength during the next year.
15. When the next Yule comes, burn the old ribbon to give the new one power.

CHAPTER 8
BONUS: CANDLE RECIPES

To finish out this book, we'll go over five candle recipes. These candles have a magical element, but they are also great candles just to have to decorate your home. You can also get as creative as you want with your candles.

ROSEMARY AND LAVENDER CLEANSING CANDLE

This recipe will fill two 16-oz jars. You can also make your candles smaller if you want, but the ingredients and instructions are written for two candles. This is a great candle to burn when you want to cleanse your space or even to cleanse yourself. It can also be used to help you go to sleep as lavender relaxes you.

You need:

- 2 large clothespins
- Wooden skewer or other utensil to stir the wax
- 2 glass jars
- Dried lavender, .5 tsp per candle – optional
- Dried rosemary, .5 tsp per candle – optional
- Rosemary essential oil, 20 to 30 drops
- Lavender essential oil, 20 to 30 drops
- Wicks with metal base, 2
- Soy flakes, 4 c
- 2 washcloths – not mandatory, but helps keep the wax from cooling off too fast

What To Do:

1. Using a double-boil or a glass sitting on top of a pot filled with some water, bring the water up to a boil. After that is boiling, turn the heat down a bit and add in the soy flakes. Stir the flakes every few minutes until they become liquid. This can take around five minutes.
2. Once melted, turn the heat off and dip the metal ends

on the wicks into the wax. Set these into the center of your jars, pressing them down with your skewer to set them in place. This will help to secure the wick to the jar.
3. After that is set in place, straighten out the wick and then use the clothespin to keep it straight and secured to the jar.
4. Very carefully, pour the wax into the jars. Something with a spout, like a measuring cup, tends to make this job easier. Drop about 15 drops of each oil into each of the jars. This is also when you would add the dried herbs to the jar if you want to use them. Then use your skewer to stir the oils and herbs throughout.
5. Wrap a dry washcloth around each jar. This helps keep the wax from cooling off too fast, which can cause cracking or shrinking.
6. Allow the candles to sit for 24 hours or until completely set. Then you can take off the clothespins, washcloths and trim the wick to an inch above the wax.

CITRONELLA CANDLE

This candle is great to use during the summer when you are doing things outside. It is a natural mosquito repellant. This will use a blend of waxes to keep it from melting in the summer heat. This will make three candles.

You Need:

- 8 oz candle tins, 3
- Citronella essential oil, 1 oz bottle
- Yellow beeswax pellets, 3.2 oz

- Soy wax, 12.8 oz
- Wicks, 3

You Will Do:

1. The first thing you will need to do is measure out your wax. The combo of waxes should be at a 4 to 1 ratio of soy to beeswax. The beeswax keeps the candle from melting as easily.
2. Next, you will set up the double boiler as we did in the last recipes and add in both waxes. Stir the wax every few minutes until completely melted.
3. As the wax is melting, get your candle containers ready. If you have wick stickers, place them on the bottom of the wick and then press it into the bottom of an eight-ounce candle tin. Do the same with the other two candle tins.
4. Once the wax has melted, pour the citronella oil into the candles and stir. Pour the wax into the pouring container and let it sit for two minutes.
5. Pour the wax into each of the candle tins. Straighten the wicks up and center them. Allow the candles to sit overnight to set.
6. Once set, trim the wick. If your candle tins have lids, place on the lid, and then label the candles.

LOVE CANDLE

This is a more advanced candle, so make sure you have gotten used to the pouring process before you try to tackle this one. This is the perfect candle to make if you plan on doing a love spell or you want to bring more love into your relationship.

You Need:

- Heart-shaped cookie cutter
- Wick and wick stickers
- Rose essential oil
- Red liquid dye, 1 oz
- 12 oz jar, 2
- Paraffin/soy blend wax, 1 lb + 8 oz
- Rubbing alcohol

You Will Do:

1. Start out by weighing your wax and then placing it into a double boiler to allow it to melt.
2. As it melts, get your jars ready. Wipe the inside of your jars with some alcohol to make sure it is free of any type of debris. Secure the wicks using wick stickers to the center of the jars.
3. Add about 30 drops of the rose oil to your melted candle wax. You can add more or less depending on how strong you would like the scent.
4. Pour the wax into a pouring container and let it sit out for a few minutes.
5. Fill the jars with the wax, leaving a couple of inches of space at the top of the jar. This is where the heart is going to go. You should have wax left in your pouring picture. You are going to need this later.
6. Using a wick bar or a clothespin, center the wick and

secure it. Set the candles aside to cool completely before continuing to the next step.
7. Once the candle from the first step is set, measure out eight ounces of wax and melt it. Once melted, add about 10 drops of the rose oil and three to six drops of the red liquid dye. Mix everything together.
8. Line a small pie plate with some parchment paper, and pour the red wax into it. Allow this to sit until solid, but not completely hard. This will take around 45 to 60 minutes.
9. Wearing gloves, take the red wax out of the pie plate and remove the parchment paper. Using a heart-shaped cookie cutter, cut heart shapes out of the red wax and set them over onto a clean sheet of parchment. Use a wick pin to poke a hole into the center of the hearts. You should be able to get about six hears out of the wax.
10. One the cooled candles, remove the wick bar and then slide the wick up through one of the red hearts and push it down to rest on top of the cooled wax.
11. Take the leftover over white wax and melt it back down. Once melted, carefully pour it around the red heart to "embed" it into the wax. Do this on both of your candles.
12. Once cooled, trim the wax and label the candle.

You can keep it to use for other embedded candles for the extra red wax you will have, turn them into small tealight, heart-shaped candles, or use them as wax melts.

YULE CANDLE

This candle is filled with the scents of the Yule season. It is a great candle to burn during Yule rituals or at any point during the season.

You Need:

- A glass container
- Winter essential oil blend
- Orange essential oil
- Candlewick
- Soy wax

You Will Do:

1. Start by measuring out a couple of cups of soy wax and melt it in a double boiler. As it melts, stick the wick to the bottom of the candle jar, making sure it is centered.
2. Once the wax is melted, remove it from the heat and mix in ten drops of the orange oil and 20 drops of the winter blend oil, and stir well.
3. Pour the wax into the candle jar.
4. Straighten the wick and secure it with a wick bar or clothespin. Allow the candle to cool overnight, and then trim the wick and enjoy.

OSTARA CANDLE

This candle is perfect for the Ostara sabbat. This can be burned during your ritual or at any time during the Ostara period to honor the sabbat.

You Need:

- A glass container
- Lavender essential oil
- Lime essential oil
- Peppermint essential oil
- Candlewick
- Soy wax

You Will Do:

1. Measure out a couple of cups of soy wax and melt them in a double boiler. You can also place the wax into a glass measuring cup and set the cup into some boiling water. Make sure the water does not come in contact with the wax.
2. Once the wax is melted, remove it from the heat and use a bit to secure the wick to the bottom of the glass jar, making sure it is centered.
3. Add ten drops of each essential oil into the melted wax and stir everything together.
4. Pour the wax into the candle jar.
5. Straighten and secure the wick and allow the candle to cool overnight. Trim the wick and enjoy.

AFTERWORD

Thank you for making it through to the end of the book; let's hope it was informative and able to provide you with all of the tools you need to achieve your goals, whatever they may be.

Candle magic is an amazing practice. Candles play a big part in a Witches life, so knowing how to use them properly within your magical practice adds so much power to a person's life. Use the spells in this book wisely. Never do a spell just because it sounds "fun." Make sure you truly need to perform the spell and fully know what you want to get out of it. Other than that, I hope you do have fun with your magical practice. With intention and purpose, these spells will never fell.

Finally, if you found this book useful in any way, a review on Amazon is always appreciated!

www.ingramcontent.com/pod-product-compliance
Lightning Source LLC
Chambersburg PA
CBHW021447070526
44577CB00002B/289